1599 Moved to Southwark nea which he and his company had recently erected.

1602 Extensive purchases of property and land in Stratford.

1602–4 Lodged with Mountjoy, a Huguenot refugee and a maker of headdresses, in Cripplegate, London. Helped to arrange a marriage between Mary Mountjoy and Stephen Belott, her father's apprentice.

1603 His company became the King's Majesty's Players under royal patronage.

1607 His daughter Susanna married Dr John Hall.

1608 Birth of Shakespeare's grand-daughter Elizabeth Hall.

1610 Shakespeare possibly returned to live in Stratford.

1613 Purchase of the Gatehouse in Blackfriars. Burning of the Globe Theatre during the première of *Henry VIII*.

1616 Marriage of his daughter Judith to Thomas Quiney in Lent for which they were excommunicated.

25 March, 1616 Shakespeare altered the draft of his will presumably to give Judith more security in view of her husband's unreliability and his pre-marital misconduct with another woman. His will also revealed his strong attachment to his Stratford friends, and above all his desire to arrange for the establishment of his descendants.

23 April, 1616 Death of Shakespeare.

1623 Publication of the First Folio edition of Shakespeare's plays collected by his fellow actors Heminge and Condell to preserve 'the memory of so worthy a friend'.

*THE PLAYERS' SHAKESPEARE*

# TWELFTH NIGHT

*The Players' Shakespeare*

MACBETH

THE MERCHANT OF VENICE

KING HENRY IV PART ONE

JULIUS CÆSAR

A MIDSUMMER NIGHT'S DREAM

AS YOU LIKE IT

THE TEMPEST

HENRY V

ROMEO AND JULIET

ANTONY AND CLEOPATRA

HAMLET

OTHELLO

RICHARD II

*Also edited by Dr J. H. Walter*

HENRY V (Arden Shakespeare)

CHARLEMAGNE (Malone Society)

LAUNCHING OF THE MARY (Malone Society)

# TWELFTH NIGHT

*Edited by*

J. H. WALTER

M.A., PH.D.

*Formerly Headmaster*
*Minchenden School, Southgate*
*Fellow of University College, London*



Heinemann

Heinemann Educational Books Ltd
Halley Court, Jordan Hill, Oxford OX2 8EJ

OXFORD LONDON EDINBURGH
MADRID ATHENS BOLOGNA PARIS
MELBOURNE SYDNEY AUCKLAND
IBADAN NAIROBI HARARE GABORONE
SINGAPORE TOKYO PORTSMOUTH NH (USA)

ISBN 0 435 19000 8


First published 1959

94 95 96 97 25 24 23 22 21 20 19

Printed in England by Clays Ltd, St Ives plc

# CONTENTS


PREFACE *page* 1

INTRODUCTION 3

TWELFTH NIGHT 17

APPENDICES:

I The Date of *Twelfth Night* 183

II Shakespeare's Theatre 184

III Music in *Twelfth Night* 188

IV Malvolio and Maria 192

# PREFACE

THE aim of this edition is to encourage pupils to study the play as a play, to see it not so much as a novel or a historical narrative, but as a pattern of speech and movement creating an artistic whole. This approach stimulates and enlivens classroom work and is also a most fruitful way of preparing for examinations.

The interleaved notes, therefore, contain, in addition to a gloss, interpretations of character, dialogue and imagery, considered particularly from the point of view of a play. There are some suggestions for acting, for the most part simple pointers to avoid rigidity of interpretation and drawn up with an apron stage in mind. Some questions are interposed to provide topics for discussion or to assist in discrimination.

It is suggested that the play should be read through rapidly with as little comment as possible. On a second reading the notes should be used in detail, and appropriate sections of the Introduction might be read at the teacher's discretion.

It is hoped that this edition will enable teachers to take the class more deeply into the play than the usual meagre allowance of time permits them to do; it is not an attempt to usurp their function.

The text is of course based on that of the First Folio, but the writings and editions of modern scholars and editors such as C. J. Sisson, J. Dover Wilson, and P. Alexander have been freely consulted and used. The text is complete. The heavy punctuation of the older school editions based on that of the Cambridge or Globe texts has been lightened. Stage directions too follow in the main those of the First Folio. The location of scenes which are usually added by editors are for reasons mentioned in the Introduction (p. 8), transferred to the notes.

My debt to Dr. L. Hotson's *The First Night of Twelfth Night* and his *Shakespeare's Motley* for material used in the Introduction and in Appendix I is very great, though it will be noted that I have not accepted all the points he puts forward. I am grateful to the Cambridge University Press for permission to quote two passages in Appendix IV from an essay in the *Companion to Shakespeare Studies*.

The Introduction owes much to the work of many scholars which, over the years, has helped to form my opinions. Among more recent writers I am conscious of the influence of Miss M. C. Bradbrook, J. R. Brown, F. P. Wilson, Sister Miriam Joseph, T. W. Baldwin, W. H. Clemen, and the work of H. B. Charlton and G. S. Gordon has been a perennial source of enlightenment.

# INTRODUCTION

## I

On Twelfth Night, the Feast of Epiphany, 6 January, 1601, Queen Elizabeth I held magnificent ceremonies and elaborate entertainments in Whitehall Palace as a climax to the traditional celebrations and merrymaking during the twelve days that follow Christmas. In the morning she went, white-robed, in procession to the palace chapel to lay on the altar her offering of gold, frankincense and myrrh, and to take communion. She dined with her nobles and guests in state. The prolonged repast, composed of some seventy different dishes, was enlivened between courses by the Children of the Chapel Royal who presented 'a show with musique and special songs' including carols. A splendid ball followed in the evening held in the Great Hall where there was also the performance of a comedy by royal command. Present at this play as the guest of honour was a distinguished Italian nobleman, Virginio Orsino, Duke of Bracchiano. On him the Queen bestowed extraordinary marks of favour by inviting him to wear his hat in her presence, to sit beside her (he insisted, however, on standing), and by chatting with him in Italian at intervals during the play. Although the title of this play is not mentioned, it seems beyond doubt that it was *Twelfth Night* (see Appendix I).

## II

In writing a play suitable to grace the revels and merriment of Twelfth Night at Court, Shakespeare bore in mind the particular qualities and styles of his fellow actors in the company. It was most important that his new play should provide them with parts appropriate to their talents. From the lists of the company's actors and the parts some are known to have taken in other plays T. W. Baldwin has made a guess at the cast of *Twelfth Night*. The star actor Richard Burbage took Orsino; the lean Augustine Phillips, who probably took Cassius and Duke Frederick, took Malvolio; the merry, peppery Thomas Pope took Sir Toby Belch; the tall thin Richard Cowley took Sir Andrew Aguecheek; Ned, who may have been Shakespeare's brother Edmund, took Viola; Samuel Gilburne, golden-haired and grey-eyed, took Olivia; the accomplished, new comedian Robert Armin took Feste; Shakespeare himself who is reputed to have played Adam in *As You Like It* and the Ghost in *Hamlet* may have taken the part of the Sea Captain or of Antonio.

For the theme he followed the old principle that a comedy should begin in trouble, end in joy, and be centred in love. This he enlarged in a way that he had developed so successfully in such earlier comedies as *A Midsummer Night's Dream* and *As You Like It*. Indeed this comedy, his last before he began writing the great tragedies, sums up the devices and methods he had tried previously. The characters are in two groups. There are a number of young men and women usually attached to the Court of a nobleman who live in a romantic world of fine courtesy, who fall in love at first sight, who observe the ideals of the chivalric code, who are impulsive, generous, quick-tempered, despairing but never broken-hearted, and who find themselves in incredible predicaments by misfortune, misunderstanding or the unreason of love. They speak in stately verse that is highly picturesque, full of comparisons and allusions to classical stories and interspersed with occasional proverbs.

Then there are the 'lighter people', the waiting-maids, servants, hangers-on, oddities, simpletons, clowns, the occasional 'purple-hued maltworm', all intensely human. Sometimes a servant will set an intrigue in motion, at other times like Sir Andrew he blunders into the main plot with ludicrous results, and again they are just humorous and laughable because they are themselves.

As for love, Shakespeare presents it in rich variety. Viola, Orsino, Malvolio, Olivia, Sir Toby, Maria, Sebastian and Antonio are all in different ways involved in love. The range is considerable, from Malvolio whose self-love congratulates itself on 'bird liming' Olivia, to Viola whose generous love like Juliet's is as deep and wide as the sea:

> the more I give to thee
> The more I have for both are infinite.

Of the other characters, while there is some doubt whether Sir Andrew has sufficient 'blood in his liver' to love Olivia, many producers hold the view that Feste loves her, and they arrange for stage business with a rose or broken lute strings to make his hopeless love plain to his audience.

For the main plot Shakespeare followed the practice of Elizabethan playwrights in adapting stories usually of Italian or French origin. On this occasion he selected a popular Italian story in which the separation of twins leads to mistaken identity and cross-wooing; this story had already been freely translated into prose and drama in French, Spanish and English. Though for the most part he drew on an Italian play *Gl' Ingannati,* 1537, and on Barnabe Riche's *Apolonius and Silla,* 1581, yet it is plain from occasional evidence in the text of *Twelfth Night* that Shakespeare had knowledge of several of the other versions. As he shows a similar knowledge of details of the background stories of *A Midsummer Night's Dream, Much Ado About Nothing,* and of the different and often obscure chronicle versions of the themes in his history plays, we catch a glimpse of Shakespeare, the man, well-read in different languages, and with a profound knowledge of the history of his own country, taking student-like care, even perhaps with his comedies, to read over all available material before constructing his own plot.

The underplot of the duping of Malvolio, and the relationships of Sir Toby, Sir Andrew and Maria he devised himself. All the characters in the play have the stamp of originality and individuality about them, they owe nothing to any source story. Even the resemblances to characters in Shakespeare's previous plays, between Sir Toby and Falstaff, Sir Andrew and Slender, Viola and Rosalind, are not more notable than their differences: Sir Toby, for whom the worst that life has to offer is an unfilled can, alongside that 'globe of sinful continents', Falstaff; Sir Andrew, who always laughs at jokes yet never understands them, alongside the empty straw man, Slender; Viola, patient, lovable, gay, alongside the brisk, confident Rosalind.

But the underplot is to provide mirth for a Christmas revel, so we have Sir Toby Belch whose wine-drinking lets loose a frolicsome, irrepressible spirit coupled with the relics of wit and education; Feste, the singer and 'corrupter of words', whose name implies the festivities in which he shares; Malvolio, humourless, vain and self-centred, a ready dupe; Sir Andrew, a butt for Sir Toby; and Maria with the sharp answers and flair for intrigue. There are roistering catches, beautiful love-songs, a clown's song; there is high-spirited nonsense; there is the nimble dancing of Feste and the capering of Sir Andrew.

There is the general topsy-turvydom traditional in the merry-making of Twelfth Night, when servants are as good as their masters and the general order of things is overturned. The too-sane steward, Malvolio, is gulled into imagining himself Count Malvolio and thence finds himself in a madman's cell; Olivia's lofty vow to retreat from the world and from men is immediately broken on the appearance of a page, Viola; the smooth order of Olivia's house is shattered by Sir Toby's uproarious midnight efforts to 'draw three souls out of one weaver'; the women, contrary to convention—but as often in Shakespeare's comedies—successfully take the initiative in their love affairs. Indeed, the men in the main plot behave as if spellbound.

Orsino is bemused by unsuccessful love into a world of fine phrases and melodies; Sebastian in meek fascination succumbs to the swift wooing of Olivia and drifts into a bewildered betrothal. All this is deftly intermingled and delicately balanced. To spice this mixture Shakespeare added an occasional topical jest: the Sophy of Persia, the new map of the Indies, the lady of the Strachy, and probably others that are now unnoticed. If Hotson is correct, he went further and presented a scandalous caricature in the character of Malvolio of Sir William Knollys, Lord Comptroller at Court (see Appendix IV).

Shakespeare binds together revelry and romance, intrigue and fidelity not only with music and song but with the recurring undertone of the sea. Apart from references to the storm that wrecked Viola and Sebastian, we are reminded in odd places by words and phrases about the sea: 'capacity receiveth as the sea', 'board her', 'hoist sail', 'hull here', 'determinate voyage', 'put to sea', 'good voyage', etc. The Duke, whose first speech introduces the themes of love, music and the sea, and whose love is 'all as hungry as the sea' brings the sea-music to a close when receiving his happiness in the person of Viola, his 'share in this most happy wreck'.

Something along these lines Shakespeare, following usual practice, submitted to his fellows in the company for their approval. That gained, he wrote a first draft of the play which he read over to them inviting comments and probably making alterations and adjustments. Thus Armin, the professional clown, author and singer, may have wished to add the concluding song, 'When that I was', with or without the customary jig. The play was then handed to a professional scribe who made a fair copy. Probably at this stage the Master of Revels censored the play and wrote his licence to act on the last page. The book-keeper or prompter then made notes in the margin of stage properties required and directions for music or noises off, he distributed the actors' parts and rehearsals began. Two things are significant about an Elizabethan play in manuscript: the scenes were not normally marked (act division was a convention established by classical drama) and in Shakespeare's plays there is hardly ever a stage direction giving a location (there are three or four but only in his history plays). Place was unimportant, the two main entrances on the Elizabethan stage might be assumed to represent two different houses, say the Duke's house and Olivia's house, or opposing countries, but usually the spectator was expected to use his imagination; in the choruses of *Henry V* he is actually urged to do so. In performance, therefore, the play flowed on without a break; uninterrupted action on the stage was essential to preserve the link between players and audience. For the same purpose Shakespeare occasionally foreshortens time or even disregards exact chronological sequence; sometimes, as in *Merry Wives of Windsor,* stories are started and left unfinished, but this failure to round them off passes unnoticed in the theatre. With the intimacy permitted by the apron or open stage, place, sequence of time, costume, and even consistency of story, are of less importance, the audience could allow themselves to be caught up into the illusion of the play. In ourselves approaching Shakespeare's plays we should bear these things very much in mind.

The company was very careful to keep the script of the play in its possession to prevent anyone from printing an unauthorized copy as had happened to several of Shakespeare's plays. *Twelfth Night* first appeared in print when Heminge and Condell, Shakespeare's fellow actors, out of their piety 'to keepe the memory of so worthy a Friend . . . alive' edited his plays in the First Folio edition, 1623. The printer used the Company's prompt copy, and it may have had the act and scene divisions marked in readiness for publication. We noticed earlier that some alterations may have been made, and there are signs of these in the play as we have it. The appearance of Fabian where we should expect Feste, the fact that Viola does not sing, although

I. ii, 57–9 suggests that she was intended to do so, and other small details, imply a change from the original design, although the reasons for the changes can only be guessed at. Existing manuscripts of Elizabethan plays indicate that there is nothing unusual in such alterations which leave uncorrected awkwardnesses and inconsistences.

## III

The stage conditions, described in Appendix II, determined to a large extent the shape of the plays, their dramatic devices, their methods and conventions.

The general lack of scenery gave the dramatist freedom to shift the scene of his play as often as he liked (*Antony and Cleopatra* has thirteen scenes in Act III), to change the scene unannounced while the actors remained on the stage (III. iv, begins in Olivia's orchard and ends in the street), or, where knowledge of locality was not necessary for the understanding of the plot, to place it nowhere in particular (where exactly does II. i, take place?). The precise locating of every scene would distract attention from the plot; the scene is where the actors are. Such imprecision coupled with the rapid two-hour flow of the play uninterrupted by scene or costume changes helped to maintain unbroken the dramatic spell.

There was a similar freedom in the treatment of time. Inevitably some scenes overlapped, but Shakespeare placed scenes out of their chronological order, he foreshortened time, or sometimes he merely confused it. When did Sebastian wound Sir Andrew and Sir Toby (V. i, 166)? They had already proved that Sebastian, whom they mistook for Cesario-Viola, was a 'devil incardinate' (IV. i; V. i, 174). The concern is not with the orderly sequence of events in real life but with the illusion of time in a play. Occasionally the passage of time is mentioned, and its touch of realism adds a depth to the play, but it may not fit in with indications of time given elsewhere in the play. (How is the three months mentioned in *Twelfth Night* V. i,93, accounted for in the play?) Shakespeare however considered it important to mark chronological order for dramatic reasons, in the choruses of *Henry V* to simulate the fashion of an epic poem, and in the speech of Time in *The Winter's Tale* to mark the balance of fathers with children, the court with the country, jealous intrigue with love and friendship.

The plays at the Globe took place in the afternoon and day-time was assumed in their action. Night was mentioned directly or by references to torches, candles, or tapers, etc., if the action demanded it, as in *A Midsummer Night's Dream* and in *Julius Caesar*, or, as in *Macbeth*, to help create an atmosphere of horror and evil.

An important convention was the practice of the soliloquy and the aside. The jutting out of the stage into the middle of the theatre floor brought the actors who were well forward nearer to the bulk of the audience than to actors at the rear of the stage. It had long been established that character and motives were announced directly, the audience was not left to guess what was going on in a character's mind. It was a simple matter, therefore, for an actor to come forward out of earshot of the others on the stage and reveal confidentially to the audience his character, his motives and his intentions. In this way Shylock and Richard III declared their villainy, Prince Hal his intention to give up his bad companions, and Olivia her love for Viola. This device linked actor and audience intimately: the spectators shared in the play, they had a god-like knowledge of the hearts of the characters, and the two things increased their feelings of tension and suspense and the moments of dramatic irony. The aside, a brief pointed remark, is often ironic, or it may give the audience a kind of nudge to remind them of some matter. It too sustains the sense of intimacy between actor and audience.

The use of boys for female parts made easy the disguising of the heroine in male dress, and the comedy, vivacity and cross-purposes that surround Viola, Rosalind and Imogen show that Shakespeare approved of it. Such a device seems clumsy and improbable to us. It is a commonplace in the romantic stories of Shakespeare's time, and one of Elizabeth I's maids of honour wore the garments of a page to visit her lover, so that the costume may have been an effective disguise. In any case the capacity for make-believe among the audience was sufficient for them to accept any disguising however absurd (e.g. Falstaff as Mother Prat, *Merry Wives,* IV. ii, 188) as impenetrable.

The ornate stage, the magnificent costumes, the royal and noble characters produced an element of formal pageantry in the performance of the plays. Gesture and stage business too were formal, dignified and restricted, and the emphasis was placed on the delivery of the speeches. To an audience accustomed to the impressive oratory of preachers at St. Paul's Cross, to sustained and eloquent speaking by its notabilities trained in rhetoric, the words of a play were particularly important. A well-spoken passage of rich word-painting, for example, reporting some event that had happened off stage was rousing and satisfying. It was a kind of pageantry in speech or as a Jacobean writer put it, 'an ampullous and scenicall pomp' of words.

## IV

The impact of dialogue was enhanced by its traditional verse-form; it gave to the major characters an impressive grandeur, a stature larger than life. In Shakespeare's plays its range, power and flexibility are truly astounding and he contrasts it from time to time with passages of prose almost as varied in style and form.

Shakespeare's verse is infinitely varied. He uses heroic couplets to form a stately narrative verse in *Richard II,* or two speakers can each speak a line of a couplet, the second speaker making a comment on the first (*A Midsummer Night's Dream,*

I. i, 196-201). A few couplets appearing in blank verse may mark an intense emotion; a single couplet may mark a wise or significant saying, or an important exit. Couplets can impart a sense of finality, of steps taken from which there can be no turning back. Couplets of shorter lines, however, are often mocking jingles (IV. ii, 112-24) though they too can be impressively final (*A Midsummer Night's Dream*, V. i, 404 ff.)

In early plays such as *Love's Labour's Lost* and *Romeo and Juliet* Shakespeare used elaborate rhyme patterns. The first words Romeo and Juliet speak to each other form the pattern of a sonnet. Such patterns employed with elaborate figures of speech are a sign of the depth and sincerity of the speakers' feelings. We are inclined to regard them as artificial and insincere, but to an Elizabethan they truly reflected the strength and complexity of the emotion described.

Prose is normally used by comic or low characters as befitting their rank, and by contrast with the verse spoken by the courtiers. It can present the stumbling conversation of a Dogberry or Verges (*Much Ado*), the chop-logic of Feste and Touchstone, the wit and expressiveness of Falstaff illuminated by vivid similes, and the power and passion of Shylock. Shakespeare's concern was always with dramatic effect. After Caesar's murder, Shakespeare made Brutus, who elsewhere spoke blank verse, utter his flat, uninspired speech to the mob as a sharp contrast to the full power of the blank verse speech he gave Antony. Why did Shakespeare make Malvolio speak in blank verse (V. i, 317-21)? Why was prose used in I. v, 152-225? In previous scenes both Olivia and Viola were given blank verse.

Shakespeare's blank verse can be elaborate, enriched with swiftly following metaphors, with similes and other figures of speech or tricks of style, and with mythological allusions; it can be plain and direct; or it can become exaggerated and violent in language in the description of warfare, in frenzied appeals to the heavens, and in boasting. Its rhythms can march with regular beat, or, particularly in later plays like *King Lear* and *Antony and Cleopatra,* the rhythms are infinitely varied to achieve the most subtle effects. The characters use the kind of blank verse appropriate to the dramatic moment and not necessarily the kind consistent with what is known of them in the play. Thus in *Macbeth* it is worth thinking over why the murderers of Banquo speak in blank verse. Again, in the same play, why should the doctor watching Lady Macbeth suddenly change from prose to blank verse after Lady Macbeth had returned to bed?

It is sometimes very difficult to understand why Shakespeare changes the dialogue from verse to prose or from one style of blank verse to another. Occasionally the changes may be due to cuts, alterations or additions made to the original play, but in general the variations are deliberately designed to achieve some dramatic effect. They should not, therefore, be overlooked or lightly dismissed in your study of the play.

## V

Elizabethan schooling provided training in rhetoric, that is the art of using words to persuade, to emphasize, and to display eloquence and wit. A most complex system of large numbers of figures of speech, devices of style and processes of thought had been formulated, and Shakespeare makes extensive use of them. While for the most part it is enough to be aware that Shakespeare's apparent spontaneous ease in writing arises from a strict training in rhetoric, a few devices in *Twelfth Night* should be noticed.

One familiar method of concluding an argument was by quoting a well-known author or book. Feste, with mock solemnity, parodies this by inventing a philosopher, Quinapalus, together with an appropriate quotation.

A good deal of amusement to an Elizabethan audience would lie in Malvolio's preposterous conclusions after he had appeared cross-gartered before Olivia. He arranges his arguments to prove that Olivia loves him according to a formula by which the truth of a matter could be established. With asinine conceit he proves the impossible in most scholarly learning.

Quite otherwise is Sebastian who uses a similar method to examine his predicament after meeting Olivia (IV. iii, 1-21). He concludes that the truth of the matter is uncertain—'There's something in't that is deceivable'. His doubts are set at rest by the priest whose presence guarantees Olivia's sanity and honesty. He accepts Olivia's offer,

> I'll follow this good man, and go with you

relying on the priest's goodness and holiness. The order of words is a clue to his thoughts, he has significantly inverted Olivia's words in l. 23.

An effort of imagination is required if we are to appreciate the importance and value of the puns that Shakespeare uses so frequently. What has been regarded in recent times as the lowest form of wit, was, as Kellett has shown, used with telling force by Isaiah and St. Paul and by the Greek dramatists. Among the Elizabethans it was an accepted means of showing intellectual brilliance and verbal dexterity. Shakespeare enlarges its scope: it may produce a simple jest or emphasize a point (Lady Macbeth's

> I'll gild the faces of the grooms withall
> For it *must seem their guilt*

is horrifyingly emphatic, it is not hysterical).

It may sharpen the irony of an aside ('A little more than kin and less than kind'); it may be a flash of bitter insight (in *Romeo and Juliet,* the gay Mercutio mortally wounded says, 'Ask for me tomorrow, and you shall find me a grave man'); and it may be employed in an exchange of witticisms.

Sometimes Shakespeare uses the two meanings of a word

simultaneously, sometimes the word is repeated bearing a second meaning, or sometimes a word may have the meaning of a word of similar sound imposed upon it. (In *Love's Labour's Lost* 'haud credo' is confused with 'ow'd grey doe', and in *As You Like It* 'goats' with 'Goths'.)

# TWELFTH NIGHT
## OR WHAT YOU WILL

### *CHARACTERS*

ORSINO, Duke of Illyria
SEBASTIAN, brother to Viola
ANTONIO, a sea captain, friend to Sebastian
A Sea Captain, friend to Viola
VALENTINE, CURIO } gentlemen attending on the duke
SIR TOBY BELCH, uncle to Olivia
SIR ANDREW AGUECHEEK
MALVOLIO, steward to Olivia
FABIAN, FESTE, a jester } servants to Olivia
OLIVIA, a countess
VIOLA
MARIA, waiting-woman to Olivia

Lords, a Priest, Sailors, Officers, Musicians, and Attendants

## *The Duke's Palace*

How will you arrange this entry to indicate the Duke's rank and his mood? Is music played before the Duke enters or not?
Is there any link between love and music?

1 *play on.* When is music played during this speech? Who is playing it? Where from?

1–3 The Duke asks for music and more music to be played until his pleasure in it is exhausted.

4 When did the Duke hear this strain?
*dying fall*, faded softly away. *fall*, cadence, closing phrase.

5 *sweet sound.* Possibly 'sweetly murmuring air'. Some critics suggest 'south', i.e. south wind, although the south wind elsewhere in Shakespeare is usually unpleasant, and Hotson refers to *Song of Solomon, iv.* 16, 'Come, thou south, and blow on my garden, that the spices thereof may flow out.'

7 Any pause here? Is the Duke standing throughout his speech?

9–14 O . . . *minute*, love is so intense, so keen in its longing, that despite its ready acceptance of countless offerings made to satisfy its hunger, the efficacy of each offering, however excellent its quality, very quickly wears away.

9–15 Is this comment on the nature of love spoken to himself or to the courtiers? Does your answer suggest a change in delivery at this point?

12 *pitch*, height.

14–15 *so full . . . fantastical*, love has such fanciful ideas that its values are more changeable than those of any other state of mind.

Which words describe the Duke's feelings: calm, moody, serene, restless, fevered, changeable, patient, tormented? According to your answers what words should be stressed, what spoken slowly or quickly? What gestures or movements are suggested?

In this speech references to music, love, and the sea introduce ideas which recur in the play.

16 What is the purpose of this? Are the courtiers anxious about the Duke? If yes, is any stage business appropriate here?
*What, Curio?* Spoken perhaps absent-mindedly.

# ACT ONE

## SCENE ONE

*Enter* ORSINO, *Duke of Illyria,* CURIO *and other Lords; Musicians*

DUKE: If music be the food of love, play on,
Give me excess of it; that, surfeiting,
The appetite may sicken, and so die.
That strain again—it had a dying fall.
O, it came o'er my ear like the sweet sound
That breathes upon a bank of violets,
Stealing and giving odour. Enough, no more,
'Tis not so sweet now as it was before.
O spirit of love, how quick and fresh art thou,
That, notwithstanding thy capacity
Receiveth as the sea, nought enters there,
Of what validity and pitch soe'er,
But falls into abatement and low price,
Even in a minute; so full of shapes is fancy,
That it alone is high fantastical.
CURIO: Will you go hunt, my lord?
DUKE: What, Curio?

17 i.e. his own 'heart'.

18–23 *Why so . . . me*. Is Curio's purpose successful? What part does the pun play in this?

19–23 When I first saw Olivia she seemed like the goddess Diana whose divine presence purifies the air from infection. Immediately I fell in love with her, and I cannot shake off my fierce longings for her, just as Acteon, turned into a hart by Diana, could not escape the pursuit of his hounds.

In classical story the hunter Acteon accidentally intruded on the goddess Diana and her nymphs as they were bathing. The offended goddess turned him into a hart, and his own hounds pursued and devoured him.

22 *fell*, fierce.

24–32 Is Valentine elderly (see I. iv. 26–7)? Is he vexed at being turned away with a message? Does the idea running through 'brine', 'dead', 'fresh', 'lasting', show Valentine's approval or contempt? Accordingly, how should his speech be delivered?

26 *element*, sky.
*heat*, course.

26–32 Which words apply to Olivia's vow: extravagant, childish, loyal, absurd, adolescent, obstinate, impulsive, silly, idealistic, ignorant, generous, unbalanced?

33 *frame*, quality.

33–9 Justify or oppose Orsino's argument.

35 *golden shaft*, Cupid's love arrow.

36–8 When her whole sweet and perfect person is utterly filled with real love.

The Duke comforts himself from a direct refusal! Which words describe his love: selfish, generous, greedy, inactive, manly, foolish, luxurious, self-pitying, self-centred, self-deceiving, unreal, true, superficial, romantic, effeminate, rapturous, sentimental, fanciful?

Is he in love with Olivia, with himself, or with love?

37 *liver, brain, and heart*. The Elizabethans believed that the blood contained three kinds of spirits or refined fluids. Natural spirits, produced by the liver, controlled such things as growth and digestion; the heart refined some of the natural spirits into vital spirits which controlled life itself; the brain refined some of the vital spirits into animal spirits which controlled what we might call the nervous system.

Love was held in general to reside in the heart, but the lowest

CURIO: The hart.
DUKE: Why so I do, the noblest that I have.
O when mine eyes did see Olivia first,
Methought she purged the air of pestilence.
That instant was I turned into a hart,
And my desires, like fell and cruel hounds,
E'er since pursue me.

*Enter* VALENTINE

How now, what news from her?
VALENTINE: So please my lord, I might not be admitted,
But from her handmaid do return this answer:
The element itself, till seven years' heat,
Shall not behold her face at ample view;
But like a cloistress she will veiled walk,
And water once a day her chamber round
With eye-offending brine; all this to season
A brother's dead love, which she would keep fresh
And lasting, in her sad remembrance.
DUKE: O she that hath a heart of that fine frame
To pay this debt of love but to a brother,
How will she love, when the rich golden shaft
Hath killed the flock of all affections else
That live in her; when liver, brain, and heart,

form of love, appetite, resided in the liver, and the highest form, spiritual love, in the brain.

38 *sovereign thrones*, i.e. places (seats) from which the different kinds of love are ruled. Notice how these words lead on to 'king' (l. 39).

## *A Sea Coast*

Some producers begin the play with this scene. Are they justified? What difference does it make?

Consider how to dress shipwrecked sailors and what belongings they might have.

3–5 What change of mood is in these lines?
How would you make it clear?

4 *Elysium*, paradise. The name Illyria has suggested this comparison.

5–7 Stress 'perchance', here used in slightly different senses, to bring out the thought.

15 *Arion*. In classical story Arion, the half-legendary poet and musician of Lesbos, was about to be put to death by pirates on their ship. Allowed to play his lyre for the last time, he then leapt overboard and was carried to land by a dolphin which had been charmed by his music.

These sovereign thrones, are all supplied and filled,
Her sweet perfections, with one self king.
Away before me to sweet beds of flowers:
Love-thoughts lie rich when canopied with bowers.

*Exeunt*

## SCENE TWO

*Enter* VIOLA, *a Captain, and Sailors*

VIOLA: What country, friends, is this?
CAPTAIN: This is Illyria, lady.
VIOLA: And what should I do in Illyria?
My brother he is in Elysium.
Perchance he is not drowned—what think you, sailors?
CAPTAIN: It is perchance that you yourself were saved.
VIOLA: O my poor brother, and so perchance may he be.
CAPTAIN: True, madam, and to comfort you with chance,
Assure yourself, after our ship did split,
When you and those poor number saved with you
Hung on our driving boat, I saw your brother,
Most provident in peril, bind himself—
Courage and hope both teaching him the practice—
To a strong mast that lived upon the sea;
Where, like Arion on the dolphin's back,
I saw him hold acquaintance with the waves
So long as I could see.
VIOLA: For saying so, there's gold.
Mine own escape unfoldeth to my hope,
Whereto thy speech serves for authority,
The like of him. Know'st thou this country?
CAPTAIN: Ay, madam, well, for I was bred and born

24ff. Viola, as a young lady of importance and good birth, naturally thinks of seeking protection at the court, but a bachelor ruler makes this difficult.

Olivia's griefs and her retreat from society raise fellow feeling in Viola's mind, and she wishes to seek service with Olivia. Olivia, however, is receiving no one, and as a last resort Viola adopts disguise as a boy and seeks service with the Duke.

43–4 until the time was ripe for revealing my state.

44 *compass,* bring about.

45 *suit,* petition, request for a favour.

46 Does the incomplete line suggest a pause in speaking?

48–9 Some villains have a handsome appearance.

50–1 How does the Captain receive this compliment?

52 Does she pay him immediately?

54–5 *become . . . intent,* fit in with my plans.

Not three hours' travel from this very place.
VIOLA: Who governs here?
CAPTAIN: A noble duke, in nature as in name.
VIOLA: What is his name?
CAPTAIN: Orsino.
VIOLA: Orsino—I have heard my father name him.
He was a bachelor then.
CAPTAIN: And so is now, or was so very late;
For but a month ago I went from hence,
And then 'twas fresh in murmur—as, you know,
What great ones do the less will prattle of—
That he did seek the love of fair Olivia.
VIOLA: What's she?
CAPTAIN: A virtuous maid, the daughter of a count
That died some twelvemonth since, then leaving her
In the protection of his son, her brother,
Who shortly also died; for whose dear love,
They say, she hath abjured the company
And sight of men.
VIOLA: O that I served that lady
And might not be delivered to the world,
Till I had made mine own occasion mellow
What my estate is.
CAPTAIN: That were hard to compass,
Because she will admit no kind of suit,
No, not the duke's.
VIOLA: There is a fair behaviour in thee, captain,
And though that nature with a beauteous wall
Doth oft close in pollution, yet of thee
I will believe thou hast a mind that suits
With this thy fair and outward character.
I prithee, and I'll pay thee bounteously,
Conceal me what I am, and be my aid
For such disguise as haply shall become

56 *eunuch,* castrato, male singer with an unbroken voice common in medieval choirs.

57 i.e. Orsino may reward him.

Is the Captain doubtful or enthusiastic? How does he show it?

59 *allow,* prove.

60–4 What is the purpose of these rhymes?

What words suit Viola: generous, gay, courageous, resourceful, ingenious, practical, mournful, a 'gold digger'?

61 Make your silence fit in with my judgement of matters.

62 *mute,* (*a*) eastern slave whose tongue was removed.

(*b*) silent person.

A touch of humour; both eunuchs and mutes were associated with eastern courts.

What are the sailors doing during this scene—standing in a row?

## *Olivia's House*

Should Maria enter first, busy about some household tasks followed a few seconds later by Sir Toby, or should Sir Toby enter first, followed closely and anxiously by Maria, as if continuing a conversation? A quick entry is necessary to sharpen the contrast of the down-to-earth, tipsy Sir Toby's views in prose with the high romantic verse speeches of the preceding scenes.

2 Sir Toby complains that Olivia's excessive grief (care) shows her fondness for death, since it is well-known that care kills people. As death has just taken away her brother, surely she should hate death and defy him by living a carefree (happy) life.

3ff. Does Sir Toby evade Maria's reproaches by shrewd wit, or is he only sober enough to pick up an odd word and misinterpret it?

6 Why can she not excuse the things she has excused before? Sir Toby echoes a lawyer's phrase.

9 *confine*, dress. Bring out the play on 'confine' and 'fine'.

10 *good . . . in.* Probably, clean enough to drink out of like the leathern drinking vessels, the blackjacks.

Is Sir Toby doing anything with his boots?

13 *undo you*, be your ruin. Does Maria pun here with a gesture towards Sir Toby's doublet, perhaps unfastened for ease in drinking? Is this going too far?

What is Maria's state of mind? Is she delighting in being pert with Sir Toby, anxious to reform him, or just a shrewish nagger?

The form of my intent. I'll serve this duke,
Thou shalt present me as an eunuch to him;
It may be worth thy pains, for I can sing
And speak to him in many sorts of music
That will allow me very worth his service.
What else may hap to time I will commit,
Only shape thou thy silence to my wit.

CAPTAIN: Be you his eunuch, and your mute I'll be.
When my tongue blabs, then let mine eyes not see.

VIOLA: I thank thee. Lead me on.

*Exeunt*

## SCENE THREE

*Enter* SIR TOBY BELCH *and* MARIA

SIR TOBY: What a plague means my niece to take the death of her brother thus? I am sure care's an enemy to life.

MARIA: By my troth, Sir Toby, you must come in earlier o' nights: your cousin, my lady, takes great exceptions to your ill hours.

SIR TOBY: Why, let her except before excepted.

MARIA: Ay, but you must confine yourself within the modest limits of order.

SIR TOBY: Confine? I'll confine myself no finer than I am. These clothes are good enough to drink in, and so be these boots too. An they be not, let them hang themselves in their own straps.

MARIA: That quaffing and drinking will undo you. I heard my lady talk of it yesterday; and of a foolish knight that you brought in one night here to be her wooer.

SIR TOBY: Who, Sir Andrew Aguecheek?

12 *tall*, fine. Possibly the original actor in this part was very tall.

80 *ducats*. A ducat was Spanish coin, worth about 6s. 8d., then in circulation in England.

What is Maria's opinion of Sir Andrew? How would you make it clear by intonation and changes in the rate of speaking?

23–4 *viol-de-gamboys*, a stringed instrument something like a violin. It was held downwards on or between the knees, and played with a bow.

*gamboys*, from Italian 'gamba', leg.

26 *natural*, like a born idiot.

Note Maria's views of Sir Andrew's 'good gifts'. Does she regard Sir Andrew with affection, alarm, contempt, or tolerance?

Are her words playful, ironic, impish, sarcastic, or bitter? Some editors think 'gust' (l. 28) is a misprint for 'gift'. What do you think?

27–8 *gift of a coward*. Is cowardice a gift? How is Maria using the word 'gift' here?

30 *scoundrels and substractors*. Difficult sounds for Sir Toby after the drink he has taken.

32–3 Does Maria speak this teasingly, archly, quizzically or roguishly?

32 *add*. Maria neatly counters Sir Toby's substractors (i.e. takers away).

In this scene Sir Toby has first defended himself by luck or judgement, then taken up cudgels on behalf of Sir Andrew, now he finds a last triumphant excuse for them both. Apart from spinning Maria round, what other actions would be effective earlier in these lines, and perhaps after 'What, wench!'?

36 *coistrel*, knave, rogue.

37 *parish-top*, a large top kept in villages and whipped as a pastime.

38 *Castiliano vulgo*. Here are two of the many explanations that have been offered of this obscure phrase:

1. Put on the grave manner of a Spanish grandee for here comes the 'knight of the doleful countenance' (Agueface).

2. I am thinking of the gold coins. A 'castilian' was a Spanish gold coin worth five shillings. Sir Andrew was Sir Toby's source of income (Hotson).

Recall what has been said of Sir Andrew's character. How should he enter: jauntily, sluggishly, mincingly, timidly, trippingly or vigorously? Is his voice bass, baritone or falsetto?

41 *fair shrew*, pretty little dear. Maria is as small as a mouse. What other meaning is possible?

MARIA: Ay, he.

SIR TOBY: He's as tall a man as any's in Illyria.

MARIA: What 's that to the purpose?

SIR TOBY: Why, he has three thousand ducats a year.

MARIA: Ay, but he'll have but a year in all these ducats: he's a very fool and a prodigal.

SIR TOBY: Fie, that you'll say so! He plays o' the viol-de-gamboys, and speaks three or four languages word for word without book, and hath all the good gifts of nature.

MARIA: He hath indeed, almost natural; for besides that he's a fool, he's a great quarreller; and but that he hath the gift of a coward to allay the gust he hath in quarrelling, 't is thought among the prudent he would quickly have the gift of a grave.

SIR TOBY: By this hand, they are scoundrels and substractors that say so of him. Who are they?

MARIA: They that add, moreover, he's drunk nightly in your company.

SIR TOBY: With drinking healths to my niece. I'll drink to her as long as there is a passage in my throat and drink in Illyria. He's a coward and a coistrel that will not drink to my niece till his brains turn o' the toe like a parish-top. What, wench! Castiliano vulgo; for here comes Sir Andrew Agueface.

*Enter* SIR ANDREW AGUECHEEK

SIR ANDREW: Sir Toby Belch! How now, Sir Toby Belch?

SIR TOBY: Sweet Sir Andrew!

SIR ANDREW: Bless you, fair shrew.

43 *Accost*, greet her with dashing elegance. A word in the latest fashion.

Does Maria hear this or not?

52–3 *in this company*, in front of all these ladies and gentlemen in the audience. Any gesture required?

62–3 *I pray . . . drink*, a gift and a kiss, if you please, sir!

*buttery*, a store room for liquor. *-bar*, a ledge across the top of the lower half of the door to the buttery.

65 *dry*, mean, stingy.

66–7 *I am . . . dry*. An allusion to the proverb, 'Fools have wit enough to keep themselves out of the rain'.

*jest*. Has anything happened to make Sir Andrew think there is a joke?

68 *dry jest*, (*a*) a stupid joke i.e. Sir Andrew himself.
(*b*) a sarcastic joke.

70 *at my fingers' ends*, (*a*) in readiness.
(*b*) she has Sir Andrew by the hand.

71 *barren*, jest-less.

73 *put down*, outwitted.

74 *canary*, a sweet wine from the Canary Isles.

Sir Andrew misunderstands brilliantly.

MARIA: And you too, sir.

SIR TOBY: Accost, Sir Andrew, accost.

SIR ANDREW: What's that?

SIR TOBY: My niece's chambermaid.

SIR ANDREW: Good Mistress Accost, I desire better acquaintance.

MARIA: My name is Mary, sir.

SIR ANDREW: Good Mistress Mary Accost—

SIR TOBY: You mistake, knight: 'accost' is front her, board her, woo her, assail her.

SIR ANDREW: By my troth, I would not undertake her in this company. Is that the meaning of 'accost'?

MARIA: Fare you well, gentlemen.

SIR TOBY: An thou let part so, Sir Andrew, would thou mightst never draw sword again.

SIR ANDREW: An you part so, mistress, I would I might never draw sword again. Fair lady, do you think you have fools in hand?

MARIA: Sir, I have not you by the hand.

SIR ANDREW: Marry, but you shall have, and here's my hand.

MARIA: Now, sir, 'thought is free'. I pray you bring your hand to the buttery-bar, and let it drink.

SIR ANDREW: Wherefore, sweetheart? What's your metaphor?

MARIA: It's dry, sir.

SIR ANDREW: Why, I think so: I am not such an ass but I can keep my hand dry. But what's your jest?

MARIA: A dry jest, sir.

SIR ANDREW: Are you full of them?

MARIA: Ay, sir, I have them at my fingers' ends. Marry, now I let go your hand, I am barren. [*Exit*

SIR TOBY: O knight, thou lack'st a cup of canary. When did I see thee so put down?

SIR ANDREW: Never in your life, I think, unless you see canary put me down. Methinks sometimes I have no more wit than

76 *Christian*, a human being, decent fellow.

76–7 *great . . . wit*. Formerly a common idea. Compare, 'beef-witted'.

85 What meaning does Sir Toby give to 'tongues'?

90 What coloured wig should Sir Andrew wear? What kind of body does 'distaff' suggest? What movements or gestures are appropriate in these lines?

90–1 *I . . . off*, I hope to see you becoming bald with the cares of married life.

99 *masques*. Dramatic performances usually in private houses in which the performers wore masks. They contained music, poetry and dancing.

101 *kickshawses*, trifles (French 'quelquechose'). Is there a pun on 'kick'?

What do you learn of Sir Toby from his use of words (confine, accost, castiliano vulgo, pourquoi, coistrel, kickshawses, etc.)?

105 *galliard*, a quick dance ending in a leap.

106 *caper*, a leap.

107 *mutton*, i.e. to go with caper sauce.

108 *back-trick*, a difficult, acrobatic, backward leap. Sir Andrew's claim to superlative ability in dancing is laughably absurd. How can this be suggested at this point? Bear in mind that he starts cutting capers later.

a Christian or an ordinary man has; but I am a great eater of beef, and I believe that does harm to my wit.

SIR TOBY: No question.

SIR ANDREW: An I thought that, I'd forswear it. I'll ride home tomorrow, Sir Toby.

SIR TOBY: Pourquoi, my dear knight?

SIR ANDREW: What is 'pourquoi'—do or not do? I would I had bestowed that time in the tongues that I have in fencing, dancing, and bear-baiting. O, had I but followed the arts.

SIR TOBY: Then hadst thou had an excellent head of hair.

SIR ANDREW: Why, would that have mended my hair?

SIR TOBY: Past question; for thou seest it will not curl by nature.

SIR ANDREW: But it becomes me well enough, does't not?

SIR TOBY: Excellent; it hangs like flax on a distaff, and I hope to see a housewife take thee between her legs and spin it off.

SIR ANDREW: Faith, I'll home tomorrow, Sir Toby. Your niece will not be seen, or if she be, it's four to one she'll none of me: the Count himself here hard by woos her.

SIR TOBY: She'll none o' the Count; she'll not match above her degree, neither in estate, years, nor wit; I have heard her swear't. Tut, there's life in't, man.

SIR ANDREW: I'll stay a month longer. I am a fellow o' the strangest mind i' the world; I delight in masques and revels sometimes altogether.

SIR TOBY: Art thou good at these kickshawses, knight?

SIR ANDREW: As any man in Illyria, whatsoever he be, under the degree of my betters; and yet I will not compare with an old man.

SIR TOBY: What is thy excellence in a galliard, knight?

SIR ANDREW: Faith, I can cut a caper.

SIR TOBY: And I can cut the mutton to 't.

SIR ANDREW: And I think I have the back-trick simply as strong as any man in Illyria.

112 *Mistress Mall's picture?* A topical allusion of some kind. Hotson suggests that it refers to Mary Fitton, one of Elizabeth's maids-of-honour, who had fallen from royal favour.

113 *coranto,* a dance with a running step.

116–7 *formed . . . galliard,* was born under the influence of a star favourable to dancing. A star within the degree of the sign of the zodiac just above the eastern horizon at the birth of a child was believed to influence for good or ill the life of that person.

118–19 Is any gesture appropriate here?

119 *dun-coloured.* A guess for the Folio 'dam'd colour'd'. Another suggestion is 'flame-coloured'.

121 *Taurus* (the Bull). The second of the twelve signs of the zodiac. The old belief was that each sign of the zodiac had power over a particular part of the body. Sir Toby corrects Sir Andrew who confused Taurus with Leo.

123–4 What suitable exit does this suggest?

124 *ha! . . . Ha, ha!* Are these laughs or a kind of *allez-oop*?

By what methods are the comic effects achieved in this scene: by play upon words, by physical characteristics, by oddities of character, speech and gesture, or by situation?

## *The Duke's Palace*

Are Valentine and Viola walking leisurely or going purposively about some business?

4 *humour,* mood, disposition.

SIR TOBY: Wherefore are these things hid? Wherefore have these gifts a curtain before 'em? Are they like to take dust, like Mistress Mall's picture? Why dost thou not go to church in a galliard and come home in a coranto? My very walk should be a jig. I would not so much as make water but in a sink-a-pace. What dost thou mean? Is it a world to hide virtues in? I did think, by the excellent constitution of thy leg, it was formed under the star of a galliard.

SIR ANDREW: Ay, 'tis strong, and it does indifferent well in a dun-coloured stock. Shall we set about some revels?

SIR TOBY: What shall we do else? Were we not born under Taurus?

SIR ANDREW: Taurus? That's sides and heart.

SIR TOBY: No, sir; it is legs and thighs. Let me see thee caper. Ha! higher! Ha, ha! excellent!

*Exeunt*

## SCENE FOUR

*Enter* VALENTINE, *and* VIOLA *as* CESARIO, *in man's attire*

VALENTINE: If the Duke continue these favours towards you, Cesario, you are like to be much advanced. He hath known you but three days, and already you are no stranger.

VIOLA: You either fear his humour or my negligence, that you call in question the continuance of his love. Is he inconstant, sir, in his favours?

VALENTINE: No, believe me.

VIOLA: I thank you. Here comes the Count.

Does the Duke sit down with Viola standing by him or sitting at his feet, or does he walk forward familiarly with her?

What words describe Viola's feeling towards taking this message: eager, reluctant, joyous, hesitant, gloomy or indifferent?

20 *leap . . . bounds,* overstep even the rules of good manners.

24 *Surprise,* captivate.

27 *nuncio's,* messenger's. Do these lines imply that Valentine should be an elderly man?

29–35 Can this dramatic irony be made more pointed by any gesture by the Duke or any reaction by Viola?

30 *Diana.* The goddess of chastity.

31 *rubious,* ruby-red.

33 *semblative . . . part,* seems as if you are playing the part of a woman—like the qualities of a woman.

34–5 *constellation . . . affair,* the star you were born under makes you a very suitable messenger on this occasion.

36–7 Should the Duke himself move here?

*Act One, Scene Four*

*Enter* DUKE, CURIO, *and Attendants*

DUKE: Who saw Cesario, ho?
VIOLA: On your attendance, my lord, here.
DUKE: Stand you a while aloof. Cesario,
Thou know'st no less but all; I have unclasped
To thee the book even of my secret soul.
Therefore, good youth, address thy gait unto her;
Be not denied access, stand at her doors,
And tell them, there thy fixed foot shall grow
Till thou have audience.
VIOLA: Sure, my noble lord,
If she be so abandoned to her sorrow
As it is spoke, she never will admit me.
DUKE: Be clamorous and leap all civil bounds,
Rather than make unprofited return.
VIOLA: Say I do speak with her, my lord, what then?
DUKE: O, then unfold the passion of my love,
Surprise her with discourse of my dear faith.
It shall become thee well to act my woes;
She will attend it better in thy youth
Than in a nuncio's of more grave aspect.
VIOLA: I think not so, my lord.
DUKE: Dear lad, believe it;
For they shall yet belie thy happy years,
That say thou art a man. Diana's lip
Is not more smooth and rubious; thy small pipe
Is as the maiden's organ, shrill of sound,
And all is semblative a woman's part.
I know thy constellation is right apt
For this affair. Some four or five attend him.
All, if you will, for I myself am best
When least in company. Prosper well in this,
And thou shalt live as freely as thy lord,

40–1 Where should Viola be on the stage as she utters this aside, and where is she in relation to the Duke?
Do they leave by different exits?

40 *barful strife,* undertaking full of obstacles.

## *Olivia's House*

While players should not be restless on the stage, some movement and gesture is required, particularly in the quick word-exchanges between Feste and Maria, to underline the points each makes. Think out some simple pattern of movements for them.

What request has Feste made to Maria before they enter? How do they enter? How is Feste dressed? Does he carry anything?

4–12 The following is a guess at an obscure set of puns:

*F.* He that is well hanged need not fear anyone's angers (cholers) or restrictions (collars).

*M.* Explain that.

*F.* A dead man will not be able to see any (colours).

*M.* A colourless sort of answer . . . That saying of yours is an army joke, for the only man not afraid of the enemy's advancing standards (colours) is a dead man.

8 *lenten,* poor, insipid.

18 *let . . . out,* the summer weather will enable me to endure it.

22 *gaskins,* breeches. What meaning does Maria put on 'points'?

To call his fortunes thine.

VIOLA: I'll do my best
To woo your lady. [*Aside*] Yet, a barful strife.
Whoe'er I woo, myself would be his wife.

*Exeunt*

## SCENE FIVE

*Enter* MARIA *and* FESTE

MARIA: Nay, either tell me where thou hast been, or I will not open my lips so wide as a bristle may enter in way of thy excuse. My lady will hang thee for thy absence.

FESTE: Let her hang me. He that is well hanged in this world needs to fear no colours.

MARIA: Make that good.

FESTE: He shall see none to fear.

MARIA: A good lenten answer. I can tell thee where that saying was born, of 'I fear no colours'.

FESTE: Where, good Mistress Mary?

MARIA: In the wars; and that may you be bold to say in your foolery.

FESTE: Well, God give them wisdom that have it; and those that are fools, let them use their talents.

MARIA: Yet you will be hanged for being so long absent; or to be turned away, is not that as good as a hanging to you?

FESTE: Many a good hanging prevents a bad marriage; and, for turning away, let summer bear it out.

MARIA: You are resolute, then?

FESTE: Not so neither, but I am resolved on two points.

MARIA: That if one break, the other will hold; or if both break, your gaskins fall.

23–5 Maria is witty at Feste's expense, but his retort that her cleverness may win her Sir Toby as a husband brings her back in alarm, lest he shall betray her secret hope.

31 Feste addresses his bauble.
*Quinapalus*, a fanciful name.

32 Olivia's first appearance should be effective. Malvolio might precede her with his staff of office, demand silence by knocking, then bow her into a seat. She might have maids-in-waiting.
How is Malvolio dressed? What is his demeanour?

33 Feste is in a desperate situation. What does Olivia's command imply will happen to him? Instead of pleading or fawning, with quick audacity he takes the tremendous risk of turning Olivia's words against herself.

41–4 Feste implies that both Olivia and himself are in the same situation: she is virtue patched with sin, and he is sin patched with virtue; i.e., they are both 'patches', or fools.

43 *syllogism*, a statement consisting of three propositions in which, if the first two are true, the last must also be true.

44 *cuckold*, husband whose wife is untrue to him.

44–5 Even as beauty must fade like a flower, so will you break the vow you have made in your great grief for the death of your brother, and, as a vow-breaker, you will be virtue patched with sin.

48 *Misprision*, misunderstanding, wrongful arrest.

48–9 *Cucullus . . . monachum*, the cowl does not make the monk.

52 These words tell that Feste has saved himself.

53 *Dexteriously*, neatly.

ESTE: Apt, in good faith, very apt. Well, go thy way—if Sir Toby would leave drinking, thou wert as witty a piece of Eve's flesh as any in Illyria.

MARIA: Peace you rogue, no more o' that. Here comes my lady: make your excuse wisely, you were best. [*Exit*

FESTE: Wit, an't be thy will, put me into good fooling. Those wits that think they have thee do very oft prove fools; and I that am sure I lack thee may pass for a wise man. For what says Quinapalus? 'Better a witty fool than a foolish wit.'

*Enter* Lady OLIVIA *with* MALVOLIO

God bless thee, lady!

OLIVIA: Take the fool away.

FESTE: Do you not hear, fellows? Take away the lady.

OLIVIA: Go to, you're a dry fool; I'll no more of you. Besides, you grow dishonest.

FESTE: Two faults, madonna, that drink and good counsel will amend: for give the dry fool drink, then is the fool not dry. Bid the dishonest man mend himself; if he mend, he is no longer dishonest; if he cannot, let the botcher mend him. Any thing that's mended is but patched; virtue that transgresses is but patched with sin; and sin that amends is but patched with virtue. If that this simple syllogism will serve, so; if it will not, what remedy? As there is no true cuckold but calamity, so beauty's a flower. The lady bade take away the fool, therefore, I say again, take her away.

OLIVIA: Sir, I bade them take away you.

FESTE: Misprision in the highest degree. Lady, 'Cucullus non facit monachum'; that's as much to say as I wear not motley in my brain. Good madonna, give me leave to prove you a fool.

OLIVIA: Can you do it?

FESTE: Dexteriously, good madonna.

OLIVIA: Make your proof.

55–6 *mouse of virtue,* dear, virtuous lady. *mouse,* a term of endearment.

57–8 Is there any change of position on the stage here?

59–64 How is this proof received by Olivia and by her attendants?

67–8 Does Malvolio speak in a frivolous, solemn, jovial, grave, or impertinent manner, or like some puritans—nasally?

69–70 Does Feste mimic Malvolio's tones? Another suggestion is that he was the actor Armin, i.e. an ermine, and therefore not a fox.

71 *fox,* sly cheat.

74–5 Note the somewhat rude rebuke and Olivia's sharp retort, ll. 81–6. How will you bring this out?

76 *stone.* Possibly a hit at Stone, a court fool.

76–7 What movement or gesture by Feste prompted Malvolio's comment?

79 *set . . . fools,* fools whose jokes are made according to a fixed pattern, are not naturally witty.

80 *fools' zanies,* clowns attendant on fools.

81–6 Olivia points out that the Clown has his proper place in society where his mocking at oddities is accepted in the right spirit, even as a prudent adviser (such as Malvolio) is not regarded as a mocker even if he rebukes faults.

83 *bird-bolts,* blunt-headed arrows used for shooting at birds.

87 *Mercury.* The classical god Mercury was, among other things, the god of lies.

*endue thee with leasing,* bestow on you the gift of lying.

Which words fit Feste, observant, malicious, agile, subtle, intelligent, loquacious?

FESTE: I must catechize you for it, madonna. Good my mouse of virtue, answer me.

OLIVIA: Well, sir, for want of other idleness, I'll bide your proof.

FESTE: Good madonna, why mournest thou?

OLIVIA: Good fool, for my brother's death.

FESTE: I think his soul is in hell, madonna.

OLIVIA: I know his soul is in heaven, fool.

FESTE: The more fool, madonna, to mourn for your brother's soul being in heaven. Take away the fool, gentlemen.

OLIVIA: What think you of this fool, Malvolio? Doth he not mend?

MALVOLIO: Yes, and shall do till the pangs of death shake him. Infirmity, that decays the wise, doth ever make the better fool.

FESTE: God send you, sir, a speedy infirmity, for the better increasing your folly. Sir Toby will be sworn that I am no fox; but he will not pass his word for twopence that you are no fool.

OLIVIA: How say you to that, Malvolio?

MALVOLIO: I marvel your ladyship takes delight in such a barren rascal. I saw him put down the other day with an ordinary fool that has no more brain than a stone. Look you now, he's out of his guard already; unless you laugh and minister occasion to him, he is gagged. I protest I take these wise men, that crow so at these set kind of fools, no better than the fools' zanies.

OLIVIA: O, you are sick of self-love, Malvolio, and taste with a distempered appetite. To be generous, guiltless, and of free disposition, is to take those things for bird-bolts that you deem cannon-bullets. There is no slander in an allowed fool, though he do nothing but rail; nor no railing in a known discreet man, though he do nothing but reprove.

FESTE: Now Mercury endue thee with leasing, for thou speakest well of fools.

101–2 *as . . . fool,* i.e. wisely. Feste alludes to the proverb, 'wise men have fools to their children'. Any gesture to accompany the compliment?

103 *pia mater,* a membrane in the brain, a brain. Here a 'head for drink'.

Sir Toby's speech, gestures and movements should not be over acted, economy in gesture and in emphasis is essential.

108–9 *A . . . pickle-herring.* A possible dietary origin for Sir Toby's family name.

109 *sot,* drunken fool.

113 *Lechery,* vile lust. This is the nearest Sir Toby can get to 'lethargy'.

116 *faith.* Better even than the proverbial long spoon for dealing with the Devil.

What changes in attitude has Olivia shown towards Feste and towards Sir Toby?

*Enter* MARIA

MARIA: Madam, there is at the gate a young gentleman much desires to speak with you.

OLIVIA: From the Count Orsino, is it?

MARIA: I know not, madam: 'tis a fair young man, and well attended.

OLIVIA: Who of my people hold him in delay?

MARIA: Sir Toby, madam, your kinsman.

OLIVIA: Fetch him off, I pray you; he speaks nothing but madman. Fie on him! [*Exit Maria*] Go you, Malvolio. If it be a suit from the Count, I am sick, or not at home—what you will to dismiss it. [*Exit Malvolio*] Now you see, sir, how your fooling grows old, and people dislike it.

FESTE: Thou hast spoke for us, madonna, as if thy eldest son should be a fool; whose skull Jove cram with brains, for—here he comes—one of thy kin has a most weak pia mater.

*Enter* SIR TOBY

OLIVIA: By mine honour, half drunk. What is he at the gate, cousin?

SIR TOBY: A gentleman.

OLIVIA: A gentleman? what gentleman?

SIR TOBY: 'Tis a gentleman here—a plague o' these pickle-herring! How now, sot!

FESTE: Good Sir Toby—

OLIVIA: Cousin, cousin, how have you come so early by this lethargy?

SIR TOBY: Lechery? I defy lechery. There's one at the gate.

OLIVIA: Ay, marry, what is he?

SIR TOBY: Let him be the devil an he will, I care not; give me faith, say I. Well, it's all one. [*Exit*

OLIVIA: What's a drunken man like, fool?

FESTE: Like a drowned man, a fool and a madman: one

126ff. Try to picture this meeting. Invent the conversation that Malvolio's report suggests.

Is Malvolio quick-witted, ponderous, lively, dull, unimaginative, simple or resourceful?

134 *sheriff's post,* a post beside the sheriff's house on which notices and proclamations were fixed.

136–41 Olivia is curious about this unusual approach, just as she was about the novelty of Feste's proof. Indicate in speaking her rising impatience with Malvolio's failure to understand her questions.

143 *squash,* unripe pea-pod. *codling,* a half-grown apple.

144 *in standing water,* at the turn of the tide.

146 *shrewishly,* (in a high-pitched voice) sharply.

draught above heat makes him a fool; the second mads him; and a third drowns him.

OLIVIA: Go thou and seek the coroner, and let him sit o' my coz; for he's in the third degree of drink, he's drowned. Go, look after him.

FESTE: He is but mad yet, madonna, and the fool shall look to the madman. [*Exit*

*Enter* MALVOLIO

MALVOLIO: Madam, yond young fellow swears he will speak with you. I told him you were sick; he takes on him to understand so much, and therefore comes to speak with you. I told him you were asleep; he seems to have a foreknowledge of that too, and therefore comes to speak with you. What is to be said to him, lady? He's fortified against any denial.

OLIVIA: Tell him he shall not speak with me.

MALVOLIO: Has been told so; and he says he'll stand at your door like a sheriff's post, and be the supporter to a bench, but he'll speak with you.

OLIVIA: What kind o' man is he?

MALVOLIO: Why, of mankind.

OLIVIA: What manner of man?

MALVOLIO: Of very ill manner. He'll speak with you, will you or no.

OLIVIA: Of what personage and years is he?

MALVOLIO: Not yet old enough for a man, nor young enough for a boy; as a squash is before 'tis a peascod, or a codling when 'tis almost an apple. 'Tis with him in standing water, between boy and man. He is very well-favoured and he speaks very shrewishly; one would think his mother's milk were scarce out of him.

OLIVIA: Let him approach. Call in my gentlewoman.

MALVOLIO: Gentlewoman, my lady calls. [*Exit*

154 What do Olivia and Maria do to cause Viola to break off her speech?

158 *con,* learn by heart.
159 *comptible,* sensitive. *sinister,* unfavourable.

165 *Are . . . comedian?* You have talked about learning your part; are you then merely an actor, a servant, and not a gentleman?

Is Olivia malicious, spiteful, venomous, ironical, contemptuous or teasing in this question?

166–7 From the bottom of my heart, no! Yet in the teeth of your slander I vow I am not what I play.

169, 170 What two meanings are given to 'usurp'?

179–80 It is madness to stay, but if you insist on giving reasons, be quick about it.

*Re-enter* MARIA

OLIVIA: Give me my veil: come, throw it o'er my face. We'll once more hear Orsino's embassy.

*Enter* VIOLA *and Attendants*

VIOLA: The honourable lady of the house, which is she?

OLIVIA: Speak to me, I shall answer for her. Your will?

VIOLA: Most radiant, exquisite, and unmatchable beauty—I pray you, tell me if this be the lady of the house, for I never saw her. I would be loath to cast away my speech; for besides that it is excellently well penned, I have taken great pains to con it. Good beauties, let me sustain no scorn; I am very comptible, even to the least sinister usage.

OLIVIA: Whence came you, sir?

VIOLA: I can say little more than I have studied, and that question's out of my part. Good gentle one, give me modest assurance if you be the lady of the house, that I may proceed in my speech.

OLIVIA: Are you a comedian?

VIOLA: No, my profound heart. And yet, by the very fangs of malice I swear, I am not that I play. Are you the lady of the house?

OLIVIA: If I do not usurp myself, I am.

VIOLA: Most certain, if you are she, you do usurp yourself; for what is yours to bestow is not yours to reserve. But this is from my commission. I will on with my speech in your praise, and then show you the heart of my message.

OLIVIA: Come to what is important in 't. I forgive you the praise.

VIOLA: Alas, I took great pains to study it, and 'tis poetical.

OLIVIA: It is the more like to be feigned; I pray you, keep it in. I heard you were saucy at my gates, and allowed your approach rather to wonder at you than to hear you. If you be not mad,

180–1 *time . . . me,* I am not a lunatic.

182–3 *sail . . . swabber . . . hull.* Viola retorts using Maria's metaphor. *swabber,* washer of decks.

184 *Some . . . giant.* How has Maria shown need for mollification? *giant,* ironical, Maria was very small. How should this word be spoken?

What action or gesture is required from Viola?

186 *I . . . messenger,* i.e. not at liberty to give my own opinion.

189–90 There is nothing threatening in my message, it is not a declaration of war or a demand for homage.

198 Olivia now unbends. She is, however, determined to enjoy herself with this interesting messenger.

198–207 Note the string of quibbles: divinity, text, comfortable, doctrine, text, chapter, heresy. Are Olivia's replies playful, mocking, jesting, thoughtful or serious? Viola is as it were unclasping the book of Orsino's 'secret soul' (I. iv, 12–13).

206–7 *Have . . . say?* Viola, at this point-blank rejection of her message, is momentarily silenced. Her change of tactics is a brilliant inspiration. What is now the topic? Is the question (l. 208) asked out of simple curiosity? Should Viola emphasize it by some persuasive action?

212 *such . . . present.* Olivia playfully commenting on the picture she has unveiled says, 'This is what I looked like at the age of—my age today.' It was the custom to paint the age of the sitter at the bottom of the portrait.

*this present,* now, today.

213 Do not over stress the last four words. Is Viola cutting, or voicing simple doubt? You should read ll. 215–16 before deciding. Notice the quick shifting of ground in these replies from the picture to the painter, and from the painter to the pigments.

be gone; if you have reason, be brief; 'tis not that time of
moon with me to make one in so skipping a dialogue. 181

MARIA: Will you hoist sail, sir? Here lies your way.

VIOLA: No, good swabber, I am to hull here a little longer. Some mollification for your giant, sweet lady.

OLIVIA: Tell me your mind.

VIOLA: I am a messenger.

OLIVIA: Sure, you have some hideous matter to deliver, when the courtesy of it is so fearful. Speak your office.

VIOLA: It alone concerns your ear. I bring no overture of war,
no taxation of homage; I hold the olive in my hand. My
words are as full of peace as matter. 191

OLIVIA: Yct you began rudely. What are you? What would you?

VIOLA: The rudeness that hath appeared in me have I learned from my entertainment. What I am, and what I would, are as secret as maidenhood—to your ears, divinity; to any others, profanation.

OLIVIA: Give us the place alone; we will hear this divinity. [*Exit Maria*] Now, sir, what is your text?

VIOLA: Most sweet lady— 200

OLIVIA: A comfortable doctrine, and much may be said of it. Where lies your text?

VIOLA: In Orsino's bosom.

OLIVIA: In his bosom? In what chapter of his bosom?

VIOLA: To answer by the method, in the first of his heart.

OLIVIA: O, I have read it; it is heresy. Have you no more to say?

VIOLA: Good madam, let me see your face. 208

OLIVIA: Have you any commission from your lord to negotiate with my face? You are now out of your text; but we will draw the curtain and show you the picture. [*Unveiling*] Look you, sir, such a one I was this present. Is't not well done?

VIOLA: Excellently done, if God did all.

214 *in grain,* fast dyed.

215– What change in word arrangement begins here? Does it suggest
19 any change in Viola's delivery? What is its intention?

Viola is bringing the conversation back to Orsino. How could Olivia bequeath the world a copy of her beauty?

220–4 Spoken lightly and mockingly as Olivia deftly avoids Viola's suggestion.

222 *labelled,* attached on a label, a codicil.

223 *indifferent,* fairly.

225 *praise,* (*a*) to flatter, (*b*) to value me.

Viola speaks passionately and forcefully.

230 *nonpareil of beauty,* perfect beauty.

Viola's verse at last persuades Olivia to reply in kind. How does she ask this question, lightly and complacently, in the mood of ll. 220–4, thoughtfully, with an awakened interest in the speaker?

231 *fertile,* abundant.

232 *groans . . . fire.* Viola has the god, Jove, in mind. To liken a man to a god was the highest praise, particularly to the majesty and magnificence of Jove, the father of the gods. (Compare *Hamlet,* III. iv, 56; *Love's Labour's Lost,* IV. ii, 119; 2 *Henry IV,* V. v, 50).

233 Olivia recovers her poise. In what way is the mood here different from that in ll. 220–4?

After a momentary weakening (l. 230) Olivia now rejects the Duke's suit a second time. Viola, in desperation lest her mission should fail, changes her approach and pleads for the Duke as if for herself.

236 *In voices well divulged,* of good reputation.

241 *deadly life,* living death. A strong phrase.

244– *Make . . . pity me.* This passage was probably spoken by the actor
52 with emphasis and energy as a kind of show piece. The short line at the end may indicate a pause before Olivia replied.

244 *willow,* a sign of unrequited love.

245 *my soul,* Olivia.

OLIVIA: 'Tis in grain, sir, 'twill endure wind and weather.

VIOLA: 'Tis beauty truly blent, whose red and white
Nature's own sweet and cunning hand laid on.
Lady, you are the cruell'st she alive,
If you will lead these graces to the grave,
And leave the world no copy.

OLIVIA: O, sir, I will not be so hard-hearted; I will give out divers schedules of my beauty. It shall be inventoried, and every particle and utensil labelled to my will: as—item, two lips, indifferent red; item, two grey eyes, with lids to them; item, one neck, one chin, and so forth. Were you sent hither to praise me?

VIOLA: I see you what you are, you are too proud;
But, if you were the devil, you are fair.
My lord and master loves you. O, such love
Could be but recompensed, though you were crowned
The nonpareil of beauty.

OLIVIA: How does he love me?

VIOLA: With adorations, fertile tears,
With groans that thunder love, with sighs of fire.

OLIVIA: Your lord does know my mind; I cannot love him.
Yet I suppose him virtuous, know him noble,
Of great estate, of fresh and stainless youth;
In voices well divulged, free, learned, and valiant;
And in dimension and the shape of nature
A gracious person: but yet I cannot love him.
He might have took his answer long ago.

VIOLA: If I did love you in my master's flame,
With such a suffering, such a deadly life,
In your denial I would find no sense;
I would not understand it.

OLIVIA: Why, what would you?

VIOLA: Make me a willow cabin at your gate,
And call upon my soul within the house;

246 *cantons,* songs.

253 *You . . . much.* What word should be stressed?

257–8 Is Olivia interested in how Orsino 'takes it'? What pauses, changes of speed and intonation should be made in this speech?

260 *fee'd post,* paid messenger.

261–4 In l. 186 Viola declines to give her own opinions. What causes her to speak so passionately here and in ll. 226–30?

265–7 Olivia quotes Viola's words. How is this shown in speech?

269 *blazon.* Two meanings are possibly implied in this word: a triumphant blast, and a coat-of-arms. 'Your speech, your features, etc., all proclaim that you are a gentleman.'

Write loyal cantons of contemned love,
And sing them loud even in the dead of night;
Holla your name to the reverberate hills
And make the babbling gossip of the air
Cry out 'Olivia!' O, you should not rest
Between the elements of air and earth,
But you should pity me.

OLIVIA: You might do much. What is your parentage?

VIOLA: Above my fortunes, yet my state is well:
I am a gentleman.

OLIVIA: Get you to your lord.
I cannot love him; let him send no more—
Unless, perchance, you come to me again
To tell me how he takes it. Fare you well.
I thank you for your pains; spend this for me.

VIOLA: I am no fee'd post, lady; keep your purse.
My master, not myself, lacks recompense.
Love make his heart of flint that you shall love,
And let your fervour, like my master's, be
Placed in contempt. Farewell, fair cruelty. [*Exit*

OLIVIA: 'What is your parentage?'
'Above my fortunes, yet my state is well:
I am a gentleman.' I'll be sworn thou art;
Thy tongue, thy face, thy limbs, actions and spirit,
Do give thee five-fold blazon—not too fast; soft, soft—
Unless the master were the man. How now!
Even so quickly may one catch the plague?
Methinks I feel this youth's perfections
With an invisible and subtle stealth
To creep in at mine eyes. Well, let it be.
What ho, Malvolio!

*Enter* MALVOLIO

MALVOLIO: Here, madam, at your service.

277 *He . . . him.* Had he?

282 *I'll . . . for 't.* What is one possible reason?

286–7 What does Olivia mean? ll. 269–71 may help.

Note the ironical, topsy-turvy change that has befallen Olivia; at the beginning of the scene she is rejecting love, by the end she is pursuing love. Is her lie to Malvolio dramatically justified?

Which of the following words apply to Olivia and which to Viola, and on what evidence: vivacious, witty, clever, changeable, moody, resolute, dignified, resourceful, sensitive, gracious, superficial, spoilt, indecisive, aimless, flippant, generous, disdainful, haughty, frank, subtle, impulsive, loyal?

From the remarks made about Olivia by Valentine, Sir Toby, and Maria in this act, it has been said that she is harsh, intolerant, a spoil-sport, aloof, impatient. Do you agree?

OLIVIA: Run after that same peevish messenger,
The County's man. He left this ring behind him,
Would I or not. Tell him I'll none of it.
Desire him not to flatter with his lord,
Nor hold him up with hopes; I'm not for him:
If that the youth will come this way tomorrow,
I'll give him reasons for 't. Hie thee, Malvolio.
MALVOLIO: Madam, I will. [*Exit*
OLIVIA: I do I know not what, and fear to find
Mine eye too great a flatterer for my mind.
Fate, show thy force; ourselves we do not owe;
What is decreed must be; and be this so. [*Exit*

## *Near the Sea Coast*

Consider this entry carefully. In what mood is Sebastian (see ll. 3–7, 17–18, 25–7, 35–6)? Can any of this be expressed in his movements and bearing as he enters and afterwards?

3–5 My birth-stars are bringing me ill-luck; the evil nature of my destiny might spread like a disease to yours.

9–10 *determinate . . . extravagancy,* I am intending merely to go for a walk.

10–13 *But . . . myself.* Any movement or gesture by either preceding or accompanying this impulsive, apologetic response?

12–13 *it charges . . . myself,* I am obliged by good manners to declare to you who I am.

15 *Messaline.* If a real town was intended it might have been Marseilles (Massiliensis).

19 *breach,* breaking waves.

Any movement or gesture here?

23 *estimable wonder,* high regard and admiration.

24 *publish,* speak openly of.

25–7 *fair. She . . . more.* In recalling his sister's virtues Sebastian's grief momentarily overcomes him. How will he show this?

# ACT TWO

## SCENE ONE

*Enter* ANTONIO *and* SEBASTIAN

ANTONIO: Will you stay no longer, nor will you not that I go with you?

SEBASTIAN: By your patience, no. My stars shine darkly over me; the malignancy of my fate might perhaps distemper yours; therefore I shall crave of you your leave that I may bear my evils alone. It were a bad recompense for your love to lay any of them on you.

ANTONIO: Let me yet know of you whither you are bound.

SEBASTIAN: No, sooth, sir, my determinate voyage is mere extravagancy. But I perceive in you so excellent a touch of modesty, that you will not extort from me what I am willing to keep in; therefore it charges me in manners the rather to express myself. You must know of me then, Antonio, my name is Sebastian, which I called Roderigo. My father was that Sebastian of Messaline whom I know you have heard of. He left behind him myself and a sister, both born in an hour. If the heavens had been pleased, would we had so ended. But you, sir, altered that; for some hour before you took me from the breach of the sea was my sister drowned.

ANTONIO: Alas the day!

SEBASTIAN: A lady, sir, though it was said she much resembled me, was yet of many accounted beautiful. But, though I could not with such estimable wonder overfar believe that, yet thus far I will boldly publish her: she bore a mind that envy could not but call fair. She is drowned already, sir, with salt water, though I seem to drown her remembrance again with more.

28 *your . . . entertainment,* the poor hospitality I have given you.
Which words best fit Sebastian: irritable, distraught, despairing, rude, indifferent, grief-stricken, self-pitying, unsociable, inconsiderate? Which words describe his speaking: slowly, quickly, abruptly, frenziedly, jerkily, with a sob in the throat, brokenly?

30–1 *If . . . servant,* I am likely to die if you will not let me be your servant.

35 *manners of my mother,* ready to weep.

38 *gentleness,* blessings.

41–2 What are Antonio's movements in making this sudden change of plan as he goes off the stage? Why does Shakespeare separate Antonio and Sebastian at this point? (see III. iii).

## *A Street*

The Folio stage direction says they enter 'at several doors'. Would you arrange this as a meeting or an overtaking?

What is Malvolio's attitude towards this 'peevish messenger'? How does he show it? Is he out of breath (see ll. 5–6)?

6 *to have taken,* by taking.

7–8 *you . . . assurance,* you should convince your lord that it is hopeless for him to think that Olivia will love him.

10 *Receive it so,* take this (message) as final, or take the ring—so (in this way, here it is).
Some stage business is required. What do you suggest?

11 *She . . . me.* Had Viola left a ring? Why does she say this? Is she lying, tactful, quick-witted, surprised, diplomatic, loyal?

ANTONIO: Pardon me, sir, your bad entertainment.

SEBASTIAN: O good Antonio, forgive me your trouble.

ANTONIO: If you will not murder me for my love, let me be your servant.

SEBASTIAN: If you will not undo what you have done, that is, kill him whom you have recovered, desire it not. Fare ye well at once; my bosom is full of kindness, and I am yet so near the manners of my mother, that upon the least occasion more mine eyes will tell tales of me. I am bound to the Count Orsino's court. Farewell. [*Exit*

ANTONIO: The gentleness of all the gods go with thee.
I have many enemies in Orsino's court,
Else would I very shortly see thee there.
But come what may, I do adore thee so,
That danger shall seem sport, and I will go. [*Exit*

## SCENE TWO

*Enter* VIOLA *and* MALVOLIO

MALVOLIO: Were you not even now with the Countess Olivia?

VIOLA: Even now, sir; on a moderate pace I have since arrived but hither.

MALVOLIO: She returns this ring to you, sir; you might have saved me my pains, to have taken it away yourself. She adds, moreover, that you should put your lord into a desperate assurance she will none of him. And one thing more, that you be never so hardy to come again in his affairs, unless it be to report your lord's taking of this. Receive it so.

VIOLA: She took the ring of me; I'll none of it.

12 *peevishly,* rudely, impudently.

14 *eye,* sight.

15–24 Viola is thinking aloud or soliloquizing. How is this made clear in speaking? Emphasize her first conclusion, ll. 20-23.

16 *outside,* appearance (disguised as a boy).

18 *her . . . tongue,* what she saw made her tongue-tied.

25–30 Viola moved by Olivia's predicament speaks with feeling on the wickedness that can arise from the deception of a disguise and the ease with which women are by nature (since Eve) deceived by appearances.

Why do ll. 29-30 rhyme?

25–6 I see how the resourceful Satan makes use of disguise to work much evil. *pregnant,* full of ideas, quick or fertile in imagination.

27 *proper-false,* handsome deceivers (i.e. men).

Which of these words describes Viola's attitude: despairing, sad, joyful, impish, roguish, vivacious, mocking, mournful, whimsical, controlled, balanced, sensible, sensitive, bright, perceptive, lively, gay?

31 *fadge,* fall into place.

32 *monster,* something unnatural, i.e. a man-woman.

32, 33 *fond, dote,* love foolishly.

MALVOLIO: Come, sir, you peevishly threw it to her; and her will is it should be so returned. If it be worth stooping for, there it lies in your eye; if not, be it his that finds it. [*Exit*

VIOLA: I left no ring with her. What means this lady?
Fortune forbid my outside have not charmed her,
She made good view of me; indeed, so much,
That sure methought her eyes had lost her tongue,
For she did speak in starts distractedly.
She loves me sure; the cunning of her passion
Invites me in this churlish messenger.
None of my lord's ring? Why, he sent her none.
I am the man. If it be so, as 'tis,
Poor lady, she were better love a dream.
Disguise, I see thou art a wickedness
Wherein the pregnant enemy does much.
How easy is it for the proper-false
In women's waxen hearts to set their forms.
Alas, our frailty is the cause, not we.
For such as we are made of, such we be.
How will this fadge? My master loves her dearly,
And I, poor monster, fond as much on him;
And she, mistaken, seems to dote on me.
What will become of this? As I am man,
My state is desperate for my master's love;
As I am a woman,—now alas the day—!
What thriftless sighs shall poor Olivia breathe.
O time, thou must untangle this, not I;
It is too hard a knot for me to untie. [*Exit*

## *Twelfth Night*

### *Olivia's House*

This scene falls into three sections, the fooling and merry-making, the wrangle with Malvolio, and Maria's plot to humiliate him. Think out the general grouping of the characters in each section and the incidental properties required.

Sir Toby and Sir Andrew are returning late fuddled with wine. Who enters first? Should they move clumsily, roisteringly, with a devil may care swagger, or stealthily but unsteadily, or in owlishly solemn discussion, oblivious of everything else, or in any combination of these?

2 *diluculo surgere* [*saluberrimum est*], to rise early is most healthy. A wise saying from a popular Latin grammar book.

1–12 This conversation has a mocking echo of the dialogues learnt by heart by Elizabethan schoolboys. Sir Toby plays the schoolmaster, but the dunce, Sir Andrew, cannot remember his simple lessons.

6 *unfilled can.* Any stage business?

8–9 *Does . . . elements,* are we not as living creatures made of the four elements. According to Elizabethan belief human beings were composed of varying proportions of earth, air, fire and water.

10–12 Sir Andrew misunderstands; he takes 'life' to mean 'way of living' or 'lifetime'. Sir Toby ironically congratulates him on this second schoolboy howler.

13 *stoup,* a large cup.

13 Does Feste bounce in acrobatically, or dance in to his own musical accompaniment, or enter in a more dignified manner with or without music? What musical instrument would he have, pipe, lute, recorder, viol (see l. 36) if at all?

16 *We Three.* A picture of two asses or of two fools with the inscription 'We Three', the spectator being the third. Feste referring to the latter picture implies that the two knights are fools, but Sir Toby quickly retorts by referring to the former picture.

17 *catch,* a round for three or more voices.

18 *breast,* voice.

21–2 *gracious . . . Queubus.* An extravagant and fantastic story told by Feste. Pigrogromitus, Vapians and Queubus are presumably made up to hint at meanings; pigro—lazy, vap—vapid, Queubus —cubus (cube) or queue. Other possibilities have been suggested.

23 *leman,* sweetheart.

25–7 There is perhaps more sense in Feste's fooling than Sir Andrew realized. Adapting Dover Wilson's paraphrase: I pocketed your

## SCENE THREE

*Enter* SIR TOBY *and* SIR ANDREW

SIR TOBY: Approach, Sir Andrew. Not to be a-bed after midnight is to be up betimes; and 'diluculo surgere', thou know'st—

SIR ANDREW: Nay, by my troth, I know not; but I know, to be up late is to be up late.

SIR TOBY: A false conclusion. I hate it as an unfilled can. To be up after midnight and to go to bed then, is early; so that to go to bed after midnight is to go to bed betimes. Does not our life consist of the four elements?

SIR ANDREW: Faith, so they say; but I think it rather consists of eating and drinking.

SIR TOBY: Thou'rt a scholar; let us therefore eat and drink. Marian, I say, a stoup of wine!

*Enter* FESTE

SIR ANDREW: Here comes the fool, i' faith.

FESTE: How now, my hearts! Did you never see the picture of 'We Three'?

SIR TOBY: Welcome, ass. Now let's have a catch.

SIR ANDREW: By my troth, the fool has an excellent breast. I had rather than forty shillings I had such a leg, and so sweet a breath to sing, as the fool has. In sooth, thou wast in very gracious fooling last night, when thou spokest of Pigrogromitus, of the Vapians passing the equinoctial of Queubus; 'twas very good, i' faith. I sent thee sixpence for thy leman—hadst it?

FESTE: I did impeticos thy gratillity; for Malvolio's nose is no whipstock. My lady has a white hand, and the Myrmidons are no bottle-ale houses.

miserable tip myself for Malvolio pokes his sharp nose into my activities; moreover my girl friend is a lady and we go to the high class Myrmidons tavern, not to mere lowdown pubs.

32 *testril,* sixpence.

35 *good life,* a life of merrymaking. Sir Andrew misunderstands again.

36 How are they grouped for the song?

What are Sir Toby and Sir Andrew doing during its course? Does Feste accompany himself? If so, with what instrument? Or does he sing it unaccompanied?

41 *Every wise man's son,* every fool. Proverbially wise men have fools for sons.

48 *sweet and twenty,* sweetheart.

51 *contagious breath,* (*a*) attractive song, (*b*) bad breath.

53 If you could hear with your nose it would be sweetness in the midst of a foul smell.

55–6 *three souls . . . weaver.* A man was supposed by the Elizabethans to have three souls, vegetable, sensible and rational; weavers and tailors, mostly psalm-singing refugees, were regarded as such miserable wretches that it took nine of them to equal one normal man. Music was supposed to have the power of drawing out men's souls, but Sir Toby proposes to raise such a shattering noise that would shock even weavers into producing three souls.

57 *dog at,* clever at.

SIR ANDREW: Excellent! Why, this is the best fooling, when all is done. Now, a song.

SIR TOBY: Come on, there is sixpence for you. Let's have a song.

SIR ANDREW: There's a testril of me too; if one knight give a—

FESTE: Would you have a love-song, or a song of good life?

SIR TOBY: A love-song, a love-song.

SIR ANDREW: Ay, ay; I care not for good life.

FESTE: [*Sings*]

O mistress mine, where are you roaming?
O stay and hear, your true love's coming,
  That can sing both high and low.
Trip no further, pretty sweeting;
Journeys end in lovers' meeting,
  Every wise man's son doth know.

SIR ANDREW: Excellent good, i' faith.

SIR TOBY: Good, good.

FESTE: [*Sings*]

What is love? 'Tis not hereafter;
Present mirth hath present laughter;
  What's to come is still unsure.
In delay there lies no plenty,
Then come kiss me, sweet and twenty;
  Youth's a stuff will not endure.

SIR ANDREW: A mellifluous voice, as I am true knight.

SIR TOBY: A contagious breath.

SIR ANDREW: Very sweet and contagious, i' faith.

SIR TOBY: To hear by the nose, it is dulcet in contagion. But shall we make the welkin dance indeed? Shall we rouse the night-owl in a catch that will draw three souls out of one weaver? Shall we do that?

SIR ANDREW: An you love me, let's do't. I am dog at a catch.

59 For the catch see Appendix III.

65 Who conducts the catch?

Does Maria enter to warn the rioters or in response to Sir Toby's call for wine (l. 13)? Which words describe her manner of entering: anxiously, demurely, timidly, flutteringly, stealthily, frantically?

69–70 Sir Toby's words imply either that he does not care in the least about Olivia and Malvolio, or, as Dover Wilson suggests, he accuses Maria of using the phrase, 'My lady' to awe him into better behaviour. 'That "my lady" of yours is a Chinese trick, we are astute enough to see through that, that "Malvolio" of yours is as worthless as the lady from Ramsey.'

69 *Cataian,* a native of Cathay (China) believed to be rogues.

70 *Peg-a-Ramsey.* See Appendix III.

The whole ballad of Peg-a-Ramsey is lost, but refrains exist in which a henpecked husband recalls his merry bachelor days and exclaims: 'Give me my yellow hose again, give me my yellow hose.' This may have some connexion with Maria's plot against Malvolio.

70 *Three merry men.* See Appendix III. Possibly all three join in.

71 *Tillyvally, 'lady',* nonsense, 'lady' indeed. Remnant of a classical schooling? (Latin titivillitium).

72 *There dwelt a man.* See Appendix III.

74 *Beshrew me,* evil befall me, strike me.

76–7 *I . . . natural,* I am more of a born fool.

78 *O, the twelfth day of December.* No other reference to this song is known.

79 Will Malvolio wear night attire, chain of office (see l. 110), and carry his staff? Will he be a figure of dignity or of ridicule? How will he see his way in the dark?

81 *honesty,* decency.

*gabble like tinkers.* Tinkers were notoriously noisy and they had, of course, their own language.

83 *coziers',* cobblers.

86 *Sneck up!* Go hang!

87 *round,* plain, blunt.

FESTE: By'r lady, sir, and some dogs will catch well.

SIR ANDREW: Most certain. Let our catch be, 'Thou knave'.

FESTE: 'Hold thy peace, thou knave', knight? I shall be constrained in 't to call thee knave, knight.

SIR ANDREW: 'Tis not the first time I have constrained one to call me knave. Begin, fool: it begins 'Hold thy peace'.

FESTE: I shall never begin if I hold my peace.

SIR ANDREW: Good, i' faith. Come, begin. [*Catch sung*

*Enter* MARIA

MARIA: What a caterwauling do you keep here! If my lady have not called up her steward Malvolio, and bid him turn you out of doors, never trust me.

SIR TOBY: My lady's a Cataian, we are politicians, Malvolio's a Peg-a-Ramsey, and [*Sings*] 'Three merry men be we'. Am not I consanguineous? Am I not of her blood? Tillyvally, 'lady' [*Sings*] 'There dwelt a man in Babylon,
Lady, lady'.

FESTE: Beshrew me, the knight's in admirable fooling.

SIR ANDREW: Ay, he does well enough if he be disposed, and so do I too; he does it with a better grace, but I do it more natural.

SIR TOBY: [*Sings*] 'O, the twelfth day of December'—

MARIA: For the love o' God, peace!

*Enter* MALVOLIO

MALVOLIO: My masters, are you mad? Or what are you? Have you no wit, manners, nor honesty, but to gabble like tinkers at this time of night? Do ye make an alehouse of my lady's house, that ye squeak out your coziers' catches without any mitigation or remorse of voice? Is there no respect of place, persons, nor time in you?

SIR TOBY: We did keep time, sir, in our catches. Sneck up!

MALVOLIO: Sir Toby, I must be round with you. My lady bade

93 *Farewell, dear heart.* Sir Toby and Feste alter the words of this song to fit their present situation. See Appendix III.

95 *Nay . . . Toby.* Is Maria anxious to prevent Sir Toby from leaving, or from further offending Malvolio, or from embracing her?

97 *Is't even so?* Does Malvolio say this in disgust, or does he believe Feste's words?

99 *there you lie.* Is there a pun here? If so, what stage business is required?

105 *Out . . . lie.* Addressed to Feste, i.e. Your last line was out of tune any rate, and you lie if you say I dare not flout Malvolio.

107 *cakes and ale,* feasting and merrymaking particularly associated with the twelve days after Christmas.

108–9 What happens to Feste in the rest of this scene?

110–11 *rub . . . crumbs,* polish your chain of office, mind your own business.

113–14 *give . . . rule,* provide wine for this ill-mannered behaviour.

115 *Go . . . ears,* be off with you, ass!

Does Malvolio withdraw with dignity, pompously, hurriedly? Is he crestfallen, humiliated, outraged, enraged, scornful, vindictive?

116–18 Sir Andrew's small intelligence befogged by wine does not grasp that he will disgrace his knighthood (*a*) by challenging Malvolio (not a gentleman), and (*b*) by running away from a duel.

me tell you that, though she harbours you as her kinsman, she's nothing allied to your disorders. If you can separate yourself and your misdemeanours, you are welcome to the house; if not, an it would please you to take leave of her, she is very willing to bid you farewell.

SIR TOBY: [*Sings*] 'Farewell, dear heart, since I must needs be gone.'

MARIA: Nay, good Sir Toby.

FESTE: [*Sings*] 'His eyes do show his days are almost done.'

MALVOLIO: Is't even so?

SIR TOBY: [*Sings*] 'But I will never die.'

FESTE: [*Sings*] Sir Toby, there you lie.

MALVOLIO: This is much credit to you.

SIR TOBY: [*Sings*] 'Shall I bid him go?'

FESTE: [*Sings*] 'What an if you do?'

SIR TOBY: [*Sings*] 'Shall I bid him go, and spare not?'

FESTE: [*Sings*] 'O no, no, no, no, you dare not.'

SIR TOBY: Out o' tune, sir: ye lie. Art any more than a steward? Dost thou think, because thou art virtuous, there shall be no more cakes and ale?

FESTE: Yes, by Saint Anne, and ginger shall be hot i' the mouth too.

SIR TOBY: Thou'rt i' the right. Go, sir, rub your chain with crumbs. A stoup of wine, Maria!

MALVOLIO: Mistress Mary, if you prized my lady's favour at any thing more than contempt, you would not give means for this uncivil rule; she shall know of it, by this hand. [*Exit*

MARIA: Go shake your ears.

SIR ANDREW: 'Twere as good a deed as to drink when a man's a-hungry, to challenge him the field, and then to break promise with him and make a fool of him.

SIR TOBY: Do't, knight: I'll write thee a challenge; or I'll deliver thy indignation to him by word of mouth.

MARIA: Sweet Sir Toby, be patient for tonight. Since the

124 *gull,* fool. *nayword,* byword.

125 *recreation,* laughing-stock.

130 *exquisite,* precise, exact.

135 *affectioned,* affected, one who puts on airs.

135–36 *cons . . . swarths,* learns passages on polite behaviour by heart and quotes them in huge chunks.

138 *grounds of faith,* firm belief.

138–60 This description of the plot against Malvolio should proceed briskly from the careful account of Malvolio's weaknesses with rising excitement to the quick, brief final instructions.

145 *complexion,* appearance, face.

147 *make . . . hands,* tell our handwriting apart.

153 *a horse . . . colour,* a trick of that kind.
How does Sir Andrew deliver his joke?

youth of the Count's was today with my lady, she is much out of quiet. For Monsieur Malvolio, let me alone with him. If I do not gull him into a nayword, and make him a common recreation, do not think I have wit enough to lie straight in my bed. I know I can do it.

SIR TOBY: Possess us, possess us, tell us something of him.

MARIA: Marry, sir, sometimes he is a kind of puritan.

SIR ANDREW: O, if I thought that, I'd beat him like a dog.

SIR TOBY: What, for being a puritan? Thy exquisite reason, dear knight?

SIR ANDREW: I have no exquisite reason for't, but I have reason good enough.

MARIA: The devil a puritan that he is, or any thing constantly, but a time-pleaser; an affectioned ass, that cons state without book and utters it by great swarths; the best persuaded of himself, so crammed, as he thinks, with excellencies, that it is his grounds of faith that all that look on him love him; and on that vice in him will my revenge find notable cause to work.

SIR TOBY: What wilt thou do?

MARIA: I will drop in his way some obscure epistles of love; wherein, by the colour of his beard, the shape of his leg, the manner of his gait, the expressure of his eye, forehead, and complexion, he shall find himself most feelingly personated. I can write very like my lady your niece; on a forgotten matter we can hardly make distinction of our hands.

SIR TOBY: Excellent! I smell a device.

SIR ANDREW: I have't in my nose too.

SIR TOBY: He shall think, by the letters that thou wilt drop, that they come from my niece, and that she's in love with him.

MARIA: My purpose is indeed a horse of that colour.

SIR ANDREW: And your horse now would make him an ass.

MARIA: Ass, I doubt not.

162 *Penthesilea.* Queen of the Amazons and presumably of large size. An appreciation of Maria's spiritedness, and a chuckle at her smallness.

164 *beagle,* a small, keen and intelligent dog, rather smaller than the modern beagle.

167–8 *Thou . . . money.* Sir Andrew is paying the bill for their carousels.

169 *recover,* obtain, win.

170 *out,* out of pocket.

172 *cut,* cart-horse.

174 *burn . . . sack,* heat some wine with sugar and spices. Is Sir Andrew reluctant to go or almost incapable of going?

## *The Duke's Palace*

1 *Now . . . friends.* The Duke greets the musicians.

How may the Duke show signs of favour towards Viola as he enters with her?

2 *but,* only, just.

3 *antique,* quaint.

4 *passion,* the pain of unrequited love.

5 *recollected terms,* elaborate phrases.

SIR ANDREW: O, 'twill be admirable!

MARIA: Sport royal, I warrant you. I know my physic will work with him. I will plant you two, and let the fool make a third, where he shall find the letter; observe his construction of it. For this night to bed, and dream on the event. Farewell. [*Exit*

SIR TOBY: Good night, Penthesilea.

SIR ANDREW: Before me, she's a good wench.

SIR TOBY: She's a beagle true-bred, and one that adores me. What o' that?

SIR ANDREW: I was adored once too.

SIR TOBY: Let's to bed, knight. Thou hadst need send for more money.

SIR ANDREW: If I cannot recover your niece, I am a foul way out.

SIR TOBY: Send for money, knight: if thou hast her not i' the end, call me cut.

SIR ANDREW: If I do not, never trust me, take it how you will.

SIR TOBY: Come, come, I'll go burn some sack; 'tis too late to go to bed now. Come, knight; come, knight.

*Exeunt*

## SCENE FOUR

*Enter* DUKE, VIOLA, CURIO, *and others*

DUKE: Give me some music. Now, good morrow, friends.
Now, good Cesario, but that piece of song,
That old and antique song we heard last night;
Methought it did relieve my passion much,
More than light airs and recollected terms
Of these most brisk and giddy-paced times.

7 The Duke is clearly expecting Viola to sing (see pp. 9, 184).
Does Viola move away from the Duke or does the Duke move to a seat? (See l. 14.)

14–15 The Duke does not realize that his words have another significance for Viola and the audience. What is this significance? Should Viola show any emotion?

17 *motions*, emotions.

20–1 *It . . . throned*, it reflects the inmost feelings of love in the heart.

22–5 The Duke is turned from his own feelings by the recognition of a fellow lover. How can this change be shown in speaking?

24 *favour*, features, face.

25 *by your favour*, (*a*) if you will allow me to say so, (*b*) like you in appearance.
Which of these two meanings does the Duke not see?

25ff. Viola's replies increase the tension. The Duke's reply (ll. 29-35), discouraging Viola may have an effect on her opposite to the one he intended. How?

30 *wears she*, gradually adapts herself.

31 *sways she level*, (*a*) holds sway steadily, (*b*) becomes on terms of equality.

32–5 In giving advice to Viola the Duke admits that men are less constant in love than women. (See ll. 93-9).

Come, but one verse.

CURIO: He is not here, so please your lordship, that should sing it.

DUKE: Who was it?

CURIO: Feste, the jester, my lord; a fool that the lady Olivia's father took much delight in. He is about the house.

DUKE: Seek him out, and play the tune the while.

*[Exit Curio. Music plays*

Come hither, boy. If ever thou shalt love,
In the sweet pangs of it remember me;
For such as I am all true lovers are,
Unstaid and skittish in all motions else,
Save in the constant image of the creature
That is beloved. How dost thou like this tune?

VIOLA: It gives a very echo to the seat
Where love is throned.

DUKE: Thou dost speak masterly.
My life upon't, young though thou art, thine eye
Hath stayed upon some favour that it loves;
Hath it not, boy?

VIOLA: A little, by your favour.

DUKE: What kind of woman is't?

VIOLA: Of your complexion.

DUKE: She is not worth thee then. What years, i' faith?

VIOLA: About your years, my lord.

DUKE: Too old, by heaven. Let still the woman take
An elder than herself, so wears she to him,
So sways she level in her husband's heart.
For, boy, however we do praise ourselves,
Our fancies are more giddy and unfirm,
More longing, wavering, sooner lost and worn.
Than women's are.

VIOLA: I think it well, my lord.

DUKE: Then let thy love be younger than thyself,

37 *hold the bent,* (*a*) be constant in direction, (*b*) stay at full pitch.

45 *free . . . bones,* carefree girls who make lace.

46 *silly sooth,* simple truth.

48 *old age,* the Golden Age of classical legend.

51 *Come away.* See Appendix III.
The positioning of the singer needs care.
Is the song 'old and plain'?

52 *cypress,* either (*a*) a coffin of cypress wood or (*b*) garlands made of cypress.

53 *Fie away.* The Folio reading which Hotson supports.

Or thy affection cannot hold the bent;
For women are as roses, whose fair flower
Being once displayed, doth fall that very hour.

VIOLA: And so they are; alas, that they are so—
To die, even when they to perfection grow.

*Enter* CURIO *and* FESTE

DUKE: O fellow, come, the song we had last night.
Mark it, Cesario, it is old and plain;
The spinsters and the knitters in the sun,
And the free maids that weave their thread with bones,
Do use to chant it; it is silly sooth,
And dallies with the innocence of love,
Like the old age.

FESTE: Are you ready, sir?

DUKE: Ay, prithee sing. [*Music*

FESTE: [*Sings*]

Come away, come away, death,
  And in sad cypress let me be laid;
Fie away, fie away, breath,
  I am slain by a fair cruel maid.
My shroud of white, stuck all with yew,
      O prepare it.
My part of death no one so true
      Did share it.

Not a flower, not a flower sweet,
  On my black coffin let there be strown;
Not a friend, not a friend greet
  My poor corpse, where my bones shall
    be thrown.
A thousand thousand sighs to save,
      Lay me, O where
Sad true lover never find my grave,
      To weep there.

70 *paid.* Proverbially pleasure was paid for with pain.

72 The Duke is quickly tired of Feste's jesting. How does he indicate this in speech, in movement, in gesture?

73 Feste is put out by the Duke's sudden change.

73–8 Does the Duke hear this? What movements are taking place on the stage? Where is Feste on the stage?

73 *melancholy god,* Saturn.

74 *changeable taffeta,* shot silk.

75 *opal.* A gem in which the colours change according to the light. *constancy,* inconstancy. Feste is ironical.

77–8 *for . . . nothing,* for it is that habit that makes a satisfactory voyage out of mere aimlessness.

81 *more . . . world,* above worldly things.

84 *giddily,* carelessly.

85 *miracle . . . gems,* her beauty.

86 *pranks,* adorns.

89 *as . . . is.* Viola cannot resist a risky phrase. How should she say it? Any alteration in pitch or speed?

93–103 When the Duke's own feelings are called in question he takes a view opposed to his advice to Viola; his general statement about men has one exception, himself.

96 *retention,* consistency, stability.

DUKE: There's for thy pains.

FESTE: No pains, sir; I take pleasure in singing, sir.

DUKE: I'll pay thy pleasure then.

FESTE: Truly, sir, and pleasure will be paid, one time or another.

DUKE: Give me now leave to leave thee.

FESTE: Now the melancholy god protect thee, and the tailor make thy doublet of changeable taffeta, for thy mind is a very opal. I would have men of such constancy put to sea, that their business might be every thing and their intent every where; for that's it that always makes a good voyage of nothing. Farewell. *[Exit*

DUKE: Let all the rest give place.

*[Exeunt Curio and others*

Once more, Cesario,
Get thee to yond same sovereign cruelty.
Tell her, my love, more noble than the world,
Prizes not quantity of dirty lands;
The parts that fortune hath bestowed upon her,
Tell her, I hold as giddily as fortune.
But 'tis that miracle and queen of gems
That nature pranks her in attracts my soul.

VIOLA: But if she cannot love you, sir?

DUKE: I cannot be so answered.

VIOLA: Sooth, but you must.
Say that some lady, as perhaps there is,
Hath for your love as great a pang of heart
As you have for Olivia. You cannot love her;
You tell her so. Must she not then be answered?

DUKE: There is no woman's sides
Can bide the beating of so strong a passion
As love doth give my heart; no woman's heart
So big, to hold so much; they lack retention.
Alas, their love may be called appetite,

98 *motion of the liver,* deeply felt love.

99 *cloyment,* cloying, over sweetness.

103 *Ay . . . know.* The Duke's words stir Viola's emotions, and for the moment forgetful of her disguise she speaks so feelingly that the Duke's curiosity is roused.

106 *they . . . we.* Viola recovers and then recklessly skates over even thinner ice. The Duke's questions increase the tension.

Notice how one idea or picture leads on to the next in these lines.

112 *damask,* i.e. red as a damask rose. *pined in thought,* brooded over it.

114–15 *patience . . . grief.* Perhaps an allusion to a description of Patience, a woman, seated on a large stone with a yoke on her shoulders and her bare feet on thorns, suffering the wounds of body and mind with a constant and quiet demeanour. This description with its moral comment occurred in a popular emblem book, *Iconologia,* 1593.

116 *We . . . swear more.* Viola changes the subject with perhaps a slight swagger.

117 *Our . . . will,* we make more of a show than our intentions warrant.

119 A very awkward question. What feelings will it rouse in the audience: ridicule, tension, awe, suspense, anxiety, curiosity?

121 *and . . . not.* A sorrowful reminder of the uncertainty of her brother's fate. Another quick recovery and change of subject.

What words fit the Duke; unstaid, skittish, moody, easily swayed, dull-witted, self-indulgent, inconsistent, passionate, self-deceiving, obstinate, weak.

No motion of the liver, but the palate,
That suffer surfeit, cloyment and revolt;
But mine is all as hungry as the sea,
And can digest as much. Make no compare
Between that love a woman can bear me
And that I owe Olivia.

VIOLA: Ay, but I know—

DUKE: What dost thou know?

VIOLA: Too well what love women to men may owe.
In faith, they are as true of heart as we.
My father had a daughter loved a man,
As it might be perhaps, were I a woman,
I should your lordship.

DUKE: And what's her history?

VIOLA: A blank, my lord. She never told her love,
But let conceaiment, like a worm i' the bud,
Feed on her damask cheek. She pined in thought,
And with a green and yellow melancholy
She sat like patience on a monument,
Smiling at grief. Was not this love indeed?
We men may say more, swear more, but indeed
Our shows are more than will; for still we prove
Much in our vows, but little in our love.

DUKE: But died thy sister of her love, my boy?

VIOLA: I am all the daughters of my father's house,
And all the brothers too—and yet I know not.
Sir, shall I to this lady?

DUKE: Ay, that's the theme.
To her in haste; give her this jewel; say,
My love can give no place, bide no denay.

*Exeunt*

## *Olivia's House*

Do they enter casually, aimlessly, with purpose, languidly, briskly, drunkenly? Who is leading?

2–3 *Nay . . . melancholy.* What have they been talking about before they enter?
*let . . . melancholy.* Almost equivalent to 'may I fry in a refrigerator'. Melancholy was a cold 'humour'.

5 *sheep-biter,* a dog that worries sheep on the sly.

7 *bear-baiting.* A form of sport in which dogs were set upon a bear chained to a post.
Apparently Malvolio, as a puritan, disapproved of the sport and informed Olivia about a bear-baiting arranged by Fabian. Olivia, too, disapproved.

9 *black and blue,* dark and livid with anger, excessively.

11–12 *metal of India,* gold, i.e. my priceless wench.
Were they expecting Maria? She enters very quickly and hustles them behind the box tree.

16–17 *make . . . him,* will fool him into fantastic imaginings.

18–19 *trout . . . tickling.* i.e. a conceited fellow who will fall into the trap if his vanity is tickled.
How Malvolio may enter is hinted at in Maria's account of his actions (ll. 13–15).

21 *she,* i.e. Olivia. *affect,* like.

## SCENE FIVE

*Enter* SIR TOBY, SIR ANDREW, *and* FABIAN

SIR TOBY: Come thy ways, Signior Fabian.

FABIAN: Nay, I'll come; if I lose a scruple of this sport, let me be boiled to death with melancholy.

SIR TOBY: Wouldst thou not be glad to have the niggardly rascally sheep-biter come by some notable shame?

FABIAN: I would exult, man. You know he brought me out o' favour with my lady about a bear-baiting here.

SIR TOBY: To anger him we'll have the bear again; and we will fool him black and blue, shall we not, Sir Andrew?

SIR ANDREW: An we do not, it is pity of our lives.

*Enter* MARIA

SIR TOBY: Here comes the little villain. How now, my metal of India!

MARIA: Get ye all three into the box-tree. Malvolio's coming down this walk; he has been yonder i' the sun practising behaviour to his own shadow this half hour. Observe him, for the love of mockery; for I know this letter will make a contemplative idiot of him. Close, in the name of jesting. Lie thou there [*throws down a letter*]; for here comes the trout that must be caught with tickling. [*Exit*

*Enter* MALVOLIO

MALVOLIO: 'Tis but fortune; all is fortune. Maria once told me she did affect me; and I have heard herself come thus near that, should she fancy, it should be one of my complexion. Besides she uses me with a more exalted respect than any one else that follows her. What should I think on't?

SIR TOBY: Here's an overweening rogue.

27 *jets*, struts. *advanced*, raised.

During these lines Malvolio in imagination has already married Olivia. Possibly he should practise the arms akimbo posture frequent in Elizabethan portraits of noblemen, and this would raise his robe or cloak while the others are speaking.

28 *'S light*, by God's light.

Do the eavesdroppers remain in position behind the box-tree throughout Malvolio's appearance? If they dodge out on some occasions, at what other places must they be careful not to distract the attention of the audience from Malvolio?

34–5 *lady . . . wardrobe*. Almost certainly a topical joke. It has been suggested that it was added to the play, and that it refers to two members of the Children's Revels Company of actors, Yeoman, the wardrobe keeper, and Strachey, one of the sharers in that company.

36 *Jezebel*, the shameless wife of Ahab (1 *Kings*, xvi ff.). Sir Andrew's scholarship again!

37–8 O . . . *him*. What actions of Malvolio call forth this remark? Should Malvolio mime his thoughts?

38 *blows him*, puffs him up with pride.

40 *state*, chair of state with a canopy.

41 *stone-bow*, a crossbow for hurling stones.

47 *humour of state*, the dignified mood of a great man, to have a mind to be the great man.

48 *demure travel of regard*, allowing my gaze to travel gravely on all round.

50 An unexpected turn in the plot is that Sir Toby overhears what indignities he would undergo if Malvolio did marry Olivia. His rage and indignation are only barely controlled by Fabian.

55 *my—some*. Malvolio was going to say 'my chain', but, suddenly remembering that he would no longer be a steward, hurriedly changed it to an appropriate adornment.

58 *drawn . . . cars*, a form of torture. The victim was tied to chariots driven in opposite directions.

How does Malvolio think he will win Olivia? By fortune, because she loves him, or because he loves her? Does Malvolio say that he loves Olivia? What kind of feeling has he towards her?

FABIAN: O peace! Contemplation makes a rare turkey-cock of him; how he jets under his advanced plumes.

SIR ANDREW: 'S light, I could so beat the rogue!

SIR TOBY: Peace, I say.

MALVOLIO: To be Count Malvolio.

SIR TOBY: Ah, rogue!

SIR ANDREW: Pistol him, pistol him.

SIR TOBY: peace, peace.

MALVOLIO: There is example for't; the lady of the Strachy married the yeoman of the wardrobe.

SIR ANDREW: Fie on him, Jezebel!

FABIAN: O, peace. Now he's deeply in; look how imagination blows him.

MALVOLIO: Having been three months married to her, sitting in my state—

SIR TOBY: O for a stone-bow to hit him in the eye.

MALVOLIO: Calling my officers about me, in my branched velvet gown; having come from a day-bed, where I have left Olivia sleeping—

SIR TOBY: Fire and brimstone!

FABIAN: O, peace, peace.

MALVOLIO: And then to have the humour of state; and after a demure travel of regard, telling them I know my place as I would they should do theirs, to ask for my kinsman Toby—

SIR TOBY: Bolts and shackles!

FABIAN: O peace, peace, peace. Now, now.

MALVOLIO: Seven of my people with an obedient start make out for him. I frown the while, and perchance wind up my watch, or play with my—some rich jewel. Toby approaches; courtesies there to me—

SIR TOBY: Shall this fellow live?

FABIAN: Though our silence be drawn from us with cars, yet peace.

76 *woodcock*, believed to be a stupid bird. *gin*, trap.

80–1 'C' and 'P' do not occur in the address that Malvolio reads aloud. No one in the audience would be likely to notice the discrepancy. It is not consistency in such matters that is important, it is the total dramatic impression.

82 *Why that.* Malvolio has called himself 'cut' or fool, and Sir Andrew's dim brain perhaps for once sees the joke and he laughs.

84 *Soft*, wait.

85 *impressure*, impression.
*her Lucrece*, a seal engraved with the head of the Roman wife, Lucretia, who committed suicide rather than survive dishonour.

MALVOLIO: I extend my hand to him thus, quenching my familiar smile with an austere regard of control—

SIR TOBY: And does not Toby take you a blow o' the lips then?

MALVOLIO: Saying, 'Cousin Toby, my fortunes having cast me on your niece give me this prerogative of speech'—

SIR TOBY: What, what?

MALVOLIO: 'You must amend your drunkenness.'

SIR TOBY: Out, scab!

FABIAN: Nay, patience, or we break the sinews of our plot.

MALVOLIO: 'Besides, you waste the treasure of your time with a foolish knight'—

SIR ANDREW: That's me, I warrant you.

MALVOLIO: 'One Sir Andrew'—

SIR ANDREW: I knew 'twas I, for many do call me fool.

MALVOLIO: What employment have we here?

[*Takes up the letter*

FABIAN: Now is the woodcock near the gin.

SIR TOBY: O, peace. And the spirit of humours intimate reading aloud to him.

MALVOLIO: By my life, this is my lady's hand: these be her very C's, her U's and her T's, and thus makes she her great P's. It is in contempt of question her hand.

SIR ANDREW: Her C's, her U's, and her T's. Why that—

MALVOLIO: [*Reads*] 'To the unknown beloved, this, and my good wishes.' Her very phrases. By your leave, wax. Soft—and the impressure her Lucrece, with which she uses to seal. 'Tis my lady. To whom should this be?

FABIAN: This wins him, liver and all.

MALVOLIO: [*Reads*]

'Jove knows I love,
But who?
Lips do not move;
No man must know.'

92 *numbers altered,* metre changed.

94 *brock,* badger, stinking fellow, 'skunk'.

98 *M, O, A, I,* Hotson suggests that these letters stand for Mare, Orbis, Aer, Ignis, i.e. Water, Earth, Air and Fire, the four elements of which the Elizabethans believed all matter to be composed. A glance at the essayist Montaigne has also been suggested.

99 *fustian,* worthless, wretched.

104 *the staniel checks,* the hawk is attracted away from the prey she is pursuing by a nearby, worthless bird.

107 *to . . . capacity,* to any normally sensible man.

112 *Sowter,* a dog's name, a 'bungler'.

112–13 *Sowter . . . fox,* the stupid fellow will follow that idea though it is glaringly obvious that the trail is false.

116 *excellent at faults,* excellent at finding the scent again after it had been lost.

117–18 *but . . . probation,* but there is no agreement in what follows that will bear examination.

'No man must know.' What follows? The numbers altered. 'No man must know.' If this should be thee, Malvolio?

SIR TOBY: Marry, hang thee, brock!

MALVOLIO: [*Reads*]

'I may command where I adore;
  But silence, like a Lucrece knife,
With bloodless stroke my heart doth gore;
  M, O, A, I, doth sway my life.'

FABIAN: A fustian riddle.

SIR TOBY: Excellent wench, say I.

MALVOLIO: 'M, O, A, I, doth sway my life.' Nay, but first, let me see, let me see, let me see.

FABIAN: What dish o' poison has she dressed him!

SIR TOBY: And with what wing the staniel checks at it!

MALVOLIO: 'I may command where I adore.' Why, she may command me: I serve her; she is my lady. Why, this is evident to any formal capacity; there is no obstruction in this. And the end—what should that alphabetical position portend? If I could make that resemble something in me, Softly—M, O, A, I—

SIR TOBY: O, ay, make up that; he is now at a cold scent.

FABIAN: Sowter will cry upon't for all this, though it be as rank as a fox.

MALVOLIO: M—Malvolio—M—why, that begins my name.

FABIAN: Did I not say he would work it out? The cur is excellent at faults.

MALVOLIO: M—but then there is no consonancy in the sequel, that suffers under probation: A should follow, but O does.

FABIAN: And O shall end, I hope.

SIR TOBY: Ay, or I'll cudgel him, and make him cry 'O!'

MALVOLIO: And then I comes behind.

FABIAN: Ay, an you had any eye behind you, you might see more detraction at your heels than fortunes before you.

124 *simulation,* way of representing.

125 *to crush . . . me,* with a little straining it would point to me.

127 *revolve,* consider.

127–30 Which are the important words needing emphasis in these sentences?

132 *slough,* snake skin, present garments.

133 *opposite . . . kinsman,* i.e. be contrary with Sir Toby.

134 *tang,* ring, clang.

134–5 *trick . . . singularity,* adopt mannerisms that single you out from all others.

136, 137 *yellow stockings, cross-gartered.* Symbols of jealousy. They were old fashioned and objects of ridicule.

138 Bring out the word 'steward'.

141 What emotions has this letter roused in Malvolio: excitement, happiness, moodiness, ecstasy, self-glorification, joy, agitation, ravishment, rapture, restlessness, fervency, infection?

In the light of the emotions you decide upon what gestures and movements would be appropriate in ll. 150–9 particularly in Malvolio's exit.

142 *champaign,* open country.

143 *politic,* political. *baffle,* disgrace (a knight).

144–5 *point-devise,* to the point of perfection.

146 *jade,* fool.

151 *strange,* stand-offish, distant in manner. *stout,* surly.

MALVOLIO: M, O, A, I. This simulation is not as the former; and yet to crush this a little, it would bow to me, for every one of these letters are in my name. Soft, here follows prose. [*Reads*] 'If this fall into thy hand, revolve. In my stars I am above thee; but be not afraid of greatness. Some are born great, some achieve greatness and some have greatness thrust upon 'em. Thy Fates open their hands, let thy blood and spirit embrace them; and to inure thyself to what thou art like to be, cast thy humble slough and appear fresh. Be opposite with a kinsman, surly with servants; let thy tongue tang arguments of state; put thyself into the trick of singularity. She thus advises thee that sighs for thee. Remember who commended thy yellow stockings, and wished to see thee ever cross-gartered. I say, remember. Go to, thou art made, if thou desirest to be so. If not, let me see thee a steward still, the fellow of servants, and not worthy to touch Fortune's fingers. Farewell. She that would alter services with thee, THE FORTUNATE—UNHAPPY.' 141
Daylight and champaign discovers not more. This is open. I will be proud, I will read politic authors, I will baffle Sir Toby, I will wash off gross acquaintance, I will be point-devise the very man. I do not now fool myself to let imagination jade me; for every reason excites to this, that my lady loves me. She did commend my yellow stockings of late, she did praise my leg being cross-gartered; and in this she manifests herself to my love, and with a kind of injunction drives me to these habits of her liking. I thank my stars I am happy. I will be strange, stout, in yellow stockings, and cross-gartered, even with the swiftness of putting on. Jove and my stars be praised. Here is yet a postscript. 153
[*Reads*] 'Thou canst not choose but know who I am. If thou entertainest my love, let it appear in thy smiling; thy smiles become thee well. Therefore in my presence still smile, dear my sweet, I prithee.'

160 Do the three eavesdroppers remain behind the box tree?

161 *Sophy,* Shah of Persia. Possibly a recollection of the journey of Sir Anthony Shirley to the Persian court, 1599-1600.

170 *tray-trip,* a game with dice in which the object was to throw 'threes'.

184 *Tartar,* Tartans, the infernal regions of classical myth, hell.

Jove, I thank thee. I will smile, I will do everything that thou wilt have me. [*Exit*

FABIAN: I will not give my part of this sport for a pension of thousands to be paid from the Sophy. 161

SIR TOBY: I could marry this wench for this device.

SIR ANDREW: So could I too.

SIR TOBY: And ask no other dowry with her but such another jest.

SIR ANDREW: Nor I neither.

*Enter* MARIA

FABIAN: Here comes my noble gull-catcher.

SIR TOBY: Wilt thou set thy foot o' my neck?

SIR ANDREW: Or o' mine either? 169

SIR TOBY: Shall I play my freedom at tray-trip, and become thy bond-slave?

SIR ANDREW: I' faith, or I either?

SIR TOBY: Why, thou hast put him in such a dream, that when the image of it leaves him he must run mad.

MARIA: Nay, but say true; does it work upon him?

SIR TOBY: Like aqua-vitae with a midwife.

MARIA: If you will then see the fruits of the sport, mark his first approach before my lady. He will come to her in yellow stockings, and 'tis a colour she abhors, and cross-gartered, a fashion she detests; and he will smile upon her, which will now be so unsuitable to her disposition, being addicted to a melancholy as she is, that it cannot but turn him into a notable contempt. If you will see it, follow me. 183

SIR TOBY: To the gates of Tartar, thou most excellent devil of wit.

SIR ANDREW: I'll make one too.

*Exeunt*

Feste enters first playing on his pipe and tabor, and probably dancing a jig between acts.

Previously Viola has shown a ready wit and a control over the direction of the conversation. Here with tact and good humour she allows Feste to exercise his talents even at her expense.

1, 3 *by*, (*a*) by means of, (*b*) beside.

2 *tabor*, a small drum carried at the side of the body.

6 *stand by*, is supported by money from.

11 *sentence*, maxim, a brief statement of an accepted truth.

12 *cheveril*, soft kid leather, easily stretchable.

Is Feste 'getting at' Viola here for her extension of his quibble?

14 *dally nicely*, play idly.

15 *wanton*, lose their meaning.

19 *wanton*, lose her reputation.

19–20 *words . . . them*. No convincing interpretation has been offered. 'Bond' has been rendered as 'broken promises', 'contracts', 'restrictions' (on stage performances by statute) and 'perjury' (by Jesuits on trial). There is almost certainly an untraced topical allusion.

20 *since . . . them*. A remark that apparently contradicts the previous opinion that words are disgraced by being too free. Viola, perhaps willingly, falls into Feste's trap, and he gleefully points out that, as they have agreed words are false, he cannot give her an answer.

# ACT THREE

## SCENE ONE

*Enter* VIOLA *and* FESTE

VIOLA: Save thee, friend, and thy music. Dost thou live by thy tabor?

FESTE: No, sir, I live by the church.

VIOLA: Art thou a churchman?

FESTE: No such matter, sir: I do live by the church; for I do live at my house, and my house doth stand by the church.

VIOLA: So thou mayst say the king lies by a beggar, if a beggar dwell near him; or the church stands by thy tabor, if thy tabor stand by the church.

FESTE: You have said, sir. To see this age! A sentence is but a cheveril glove to a good wit: how quickly the wrong side may be turned outward.

VIOLA: Nay, that's certain; they that dally nicely with words may quickly make them wanton.

FESTE: I would, therefore, my sister had had no name, sir.

VIOLA: Why, man?

FESTE: Why, sir, her name's a word, and to dally with that word might make my sister wanton. But indeed, words are very rascals since bonds disgraced them.

VIOLA: Thy reason, man?

FESTE: Troth, sir, I can yield you none without words, and words are grown so false, I am loath to prove reason with them.

VIOLA: I warrant thou art a merry fellow and carest for nothing.

FESTE: Not so, sir, I do care for something; but in my con-

29 *make you invisible,* an invitation to Viola to go away.

37 *but,* if . . . not.

39 *your wisdom.* A sarcastic suggestion that Viola is a fool.

40 *pass upon,* make a fool of.

42 *commodity,* bundle, rag-bag.

47 *Would . . . bred?* Any gesture required?

48 *use,* interest.

49 *Pandarus.* Meetings between the lovers Troilus, son of King Priam of Troy, and Cressida were arranged by Pandarus, Cressida's uncle. Cressida was later sent to the Greek besiegers as a hostage, and she lost no time in accepting the love of the Greek warrior Deiphobus. In her old age, cast off by Deiphobus, smitten by leprosy, she was reduced to miserable beggary. The story was a popular one, and was told by Chaucer and dramatized by Shakespeare in *Troilus and Cressida.*

49–50 There is also the hint that if he is further tipped he will arrange a meeting between Viola and Olivia and thus play Pandarus in another sense. Viola takes the hint.

54 *construe,* explain.

54–5 *who . . . welkin.* Feste has a suspicion that Viola is not what she appears to be.

55 *welkin . . . 'element'.* The train of thought is, 'Perhaps I should say "element", but the word has been over-used, and I am obliged to use that fantastic word "welkin". Both words mean "sky" or "sphere".'

58 *wit,* intelligence.

60 *quality,* rank.

61 *haggard,* untrained hawk. *check at,* swerves aside after.

science, sir, I do not care for you. If that be to care for nothing, sir, I would it would make you invisible.

VIOLA: Art not thou the Lady Olivia's fool?

FESTE: No indeed, sir, the Lady Olivia has no folly; she will keep no fool, sir, till she be married; and fools are as like husbands as pilchards are to herrings—the husband's the bigger. I am indeed not her fool, but her corrupter of words.

VIOLA: I saw thee late at the Count Orsino's.

FESTE: Foolery, sir, does walk about the orb like the sun, it shines every where. I would be sorry, sir, but the fool should be as oft with your master as with my mistress: I think I saw your wisdom there.

VIOLA: Nay, an thou pass upon me, I'll no more with thee. Hold, there's expenses for thee.

FESTE: Now Jove in his next commodity of hair send thee a beard.

VIOLA: By my troth, I'll tell thee, I am almost sick for one; [*Aside*] though I would not have it grow on my chin. Is thy lady within?

FESTE: Would not a pair of these have bred, sir?

VIOLA: Yes, being kept together and put to use.

FESTE: I would play Lord Pandarus of Phrygia, sir, to bring a Cressida to this Troilus.

VIOLA: I understand you, sir; 'tis well begged.

FESTE: The matter, I hope, is not great, sir, begging but a beggar: Cressida was a beggar. My lady is within, sir. I will construe to them whence you come; who you are and what you would are out of my welkin—I might say 'element', but the word is over-worn. [*Exit*

VIOLA: This fellow is wise enough to play the fool,
And to do that well craves a kind of wit.
He must observe their mood on whom he jests,
The quality of persons, and the time;
And, like the haggard, check at every feather

64–5 *For folly . . . wit,* the folly that Feste speaks reveals his wisdom and is acceptable and right; but the wise men who talk foolishly only injure their reputation for wisdom.

While Olivia defends Feste, only Viola speaks with such sympathetic understanding and appreciation of him. These lines not only compliment Feste, but they show Viola's perception and tenderness.

66, 68 Sir Toby and Sir Andrew greet Viola with mockingly extravagant courtesy and affected speech.

71 *encounter.* An affected way of saying 'go to'.

72 *trade,* (*a*) course, (*b*) business.

73 *bound,* (*a*) obliged, (*b*) sailing on the way.

Viola takes up the word 'trade' and enlarges the idea.

*list,* aim, goal.

75 *taste,* i.e. test, try out.

79 *gait,* (*a*) going, (*b*) gate. Viola's punning retort to Sir Toby's 'go', 'enter'.

80 *prevented,* anticipated, forestalled.

With what gestures does Viola greet Olivia?

81–6 *Most . . . ear.* Viola speaks in a high flown, complimentary style of a courtier to his lady when she speaks as the Count's messenger.

86 *pregnant,* ready, quick in understanding. *vouchsafed,* attentive.

How does Sir Andrew get them 'all ready'?

90–91 *Give . . . hand.* Viola leads Olivia and bows her into a seat.

That comes before his eye. This is a practice
As full of labour as a wise man's art;
For folly that he wisely shows is fit,
But wise men, folly-fall'n, quite taint their wit.

*Enter* SIR TOBY, *and* SIR ANDREW

SIR TOBY: Save you, gentleman.

VIOLA: And you, sir.

SIR ANDREW: Dieu vous garde, monsieur.

VIOLA: Et vous aussi, votre serviteur.

SIR ANDREW: I hope, sir, you are; and I am yours.

SIR TOBY: Will you encounter the house? My niece is desirous you should enter, if your trade be to her.

VIOLA: I am bound to your niece, sir; I mean she is the list of my voyage.

SIR TOBY: Taste your legs, sir, put them to motion.

VIOLA: My legs do better understand me, sir, than I understand what you mean by bidding me taste my legs.

SIR TOBY: I mean, to go, sir, to enter.

VIOLA: I will answer you with gait and entrance. But we are prevented.

*Enter* OLIVIA *and* MARIA

Most excellent accomplished lady, the heavens rain odours on you.

SIR ANDREW: That youth's a rare courtier—'Rain odours', well.

VIOLA: My matter hath no voice, lady, but to your own most pregnant and vouchsafed ear.

SIR ANDREW: 'Odours', 'pregnant' and 'vouchsafed'—I'll get 'em all three all ready.

OLIVIA: Let the garden door be shut, and leave me to my hearing. [*Exeunt Sir Toby, Sir Andrew, and Maria*] Give me your hand, sir.

96 *lowly feigning,* sham lowliness.

105 *suit,* make love for someone else.

107 *music from the spheres.* The Greek philosopher Pythagoras put forward the theory that the universe consisted of eight hollow spheres in which the stars and planets were variously fixed. The spheres revolved round the Earth at the centre, each producing a note which combined with the notes from the other spheres to produce perfect harmony—inaudible to human beings.

108– Olivia was so much under the spell of Viola during the previous
14 visit that she acted on a disgraceful impulse in sending the ring. For that she is ashamed.

110 *abuse,* wrong, deceive.

112 *Under . . . sit,* I must bear the harsh opinion you have of me.

115– My sense of honour is being attacked by all the desires that the
17 overmastering passion of love lets loose.

117 *receiving,* quick mind, understanding.

118 *cypress,* black gauze used for mourning. Viola can see through the outward expression of grief to the intense love in Olivia's heart which has caused it.

121 *grize,* step.

*vulgar proof,* common knowledge.

VIOLA: My duty, madam, and most humble service.
OLIVIA: What is your name?
VIOLA: Cesario is your servant's name, fair princess.
OLIVIA: My servant, sir? 'Twas never merry world
Since lowly feigning was called compliment.
You're servant to the Count Orsino, youth.
VIOLA: And he is yours, and his must needs be yours:
Your servant's servant is your servant, madam.
OLIVIA: For him, I think not on him; for his thoughts,
Would they were blanks rather than filled with me.
VIOLA: Madam, I come to whet your gentle thoughts
On his behalf.
OLIVIA: O, by your leave, I pray you.
I bade you never speak again of him;
But would you undertake another suit,
I had rather hear you to solicit that
Than music from the spheres.
VIOLA: Dear lady—
OLIVIA: Give me leave, beseech you. I did send,
After the last enchantment you did here,
A ring in chase of you. So did I abuse
Myself, my servant, and, I fear me, you.
Under your hard construction must I sit,
To force that on you in a shameful cunning
Which you knew none of yours. What might you think?
Have you not set mine honour at the stake,
And baited it with all th' unmuzzled thoughts
That tyrannous heart can think? To one of your receiving
Enough is shown; a cypress, not a bosom,
Hides my heart. So, let me hear you speak.
VIOLA: I pity you.
OLIVIA: That's a degree to love.
VIOLA: No, not a grize; for 'tis a vulgar proof
That very oft we pity enemies.

123ff. Olivia makes a tremendous effort to control her feelings and recover her dignity. She comments perhaps bitterly that poor people like Viola are all too often proud, and that it would be far better to be rejected by a nobleman than despised by a servant.

128 Another effort at control.

129–30 *And yet . . . man.* Her admiration for Viola springs to her lips in spite of her self-control.

130 *proper,* fine.

131 *due west.* Olivia implies that the episode of her love for Viola is now finished.

132 *Westward ho.* The cry of Thames' watermen ready to row up stream.

Olivia has apparently mastered her feelings and the scene is about to close, but Viola's question takes her off her guard and she pleads for some crumb of comfort.

137–8 *That . . . of you,* that you forget your position in offering love to a servant. If I do, I also forget your position and imagine you to be what you are not.

142 *your fool,* i.e. you are trifling with me, making my pains as messenger good for nothing.

Olivia had not answered Viola's question (l. 134) nor had she allowed her to deliver her message.

147ff. Olivia's feelings overwhelm her. What effect will this have on her speech and breathing? Why does she suddenly use 'thee' and 'thou' instead of 'you'?

149 *maugre,* in spite of.

151–3 Do not persuade yourself from what I have said that because I woo you (against my reason) you have no reason to woo me. Such an argument you should overrule by a further reason . . . .

156 *one heart . . . truth,* one love, one affection, one devotion.

145–62 Why is rhyme used here: to mark the ending of the scene; absentmindedness on Shakespeare's part; to preserve the dignity of two violently impassioned people; to emphasize the intense feeling at the climax of the scene?

Olivia's state is completely reversed, not only is she in love, she is pleading helplessly and is rejected.

Which words apply to Olivia: imperious, impulsive, frank, petty, petulant, spoilt, wilful, dignified, decorous, passionate, honest?

OLIVIA: Why, then, methinks 'tis time to smile again.
O world, how apt the poor are to be proud.
If one should be a prey, how much the better
To fall before the lion than the wolf. [*Clock strikes*
The clock upbraids me with the waste of time.
Be not afraid, good youth, I will not have you;
And yet, when wit and youth is come to harvest,
Your wife is like to reap a proper man.
There lies your way, due west.

VIOLA: Then 'Westward-ho!'
Grace and good disposition attend your ladyship.
You'll nothing, madam, to my lord by me?

OLIVIA: Stay.
I prithee tell me what thou think'st of me.

VIOLA: That you do think you are not what you are.

OLIVIA: If I think so, I think the same of you.

VIOLA: Then think you right: I am not what I am.

OLIVIA: I would you were as I would have you be.

VIOLA: Would it be better, madam, than I am?
I wish it might, for now I am your fool.

OLIVIA: O, what a deal of scorn looks beautiful
In the contempt and anger of his lip.
A murderous guilt shows not itself more soon
Than love that would seem hid. Love's night is noon;
Cesario, by the roses of the spring,
By maidhood, honour, truth and everything,
I love thee so that, maugre all thy pride,
Nor wit nor reason can my passion hide.
Do not extort thy reasons from this clause,
For that I woo, thou therefore hast no cause;
But rather reason thus with reason fetter:
Love sought is good, but given unsought is better.

VIOLA: By innocence I swear, and by my youth,
I have one heart, one bosom, and one truth,

## *Olivia's House*

Who enters first?

2 Sir Andrew has been spitting out bad-tempered remarks. What is Shakespeare preparing for in making him annoyed?
*venom.* He is obviously in a furious anger and ready to provoke a quarrel, as Maria said of him earlier.

9 *argument,* evidence, proof.

11–12 *oaths of judgement and reason.* Dover Wilson notes that three conditions were necessary for the swearing of an oath: truth, judgement and justice. Fabian purposely omits 'truth'.

13 *grand-jurymen,* members of a grand jury, a body of men who enquired into the cases to be tried to decide whether the evidence was sufficient for the trial to go forward.

15ff. Sir Andrew's suspicions are lulled, and by the end of this speech he is ready for any folly. How should he show this change?

20 *balked,* missed.

And that no woman has, nor never none
Shall mistress be of it, save I alone.
And so adieu, good madam; nevermore
Will I my master's tears to you deplore.

OLIVIA: Yet come again; for thou perhaps mayst move
That heart which now abhors to like his love.

*Exeunt*

## SCENE TWO

*Enter* SIR TOBY, SIR ANDREW, *and* FABIAN

SIR ANDREW: No, faith, I'll not stay a jot longer.

SIR TOBY: Thy reason, dear venom, give thy reason.

FABIAN: You must needs yield your reason, Sir Andrew.

SIR ANDREW: Marry, I saw your niece do more favours to the Count's serving-man than ever she bestowed upon me; I saw't i' the orchard.

SIR TOBY: Did she see thee the while, old boy? Tell me that.

SIR ANDREW: As plain as I see you now.

FABIAN: This was a great argument of love in her toward you.

SIR ANDREW: 'S light, will you make an ass o' me?

FABIAN: I will prove it legitimate, sir, upon the oaths of judgement and reason.

SIR TOBY: And they have been grand-jurymen since before Noah was a sailor.

FABIAN: She did show favour to the youth in your sight only to exasperate you, to awake your dormouse valour, to put fire in your heart and brimstone in your liver. You should then have accosted her, and with some excellent jests, fire-new from the mint, you should have banged the youth into dumbness. This was looked for at your hand, and this was balked.

21 *double gilt,* a dish or vessel twice plated with gold, i.e. a doubly golden opportunity.

22 *you . . . opinion,* my lady now regards you with cold disfavour.

23 *Dutchman's beard.* Possibly Shakespeare had in mind the voyage of the Dutchman, William Barentz, whose expedition sailed round northern Nova Zembla in 1596.

25 *policy,* scheming, intrigue.

27 *Brownist,* a member of a Puritan sect, the Independents, founded by Robert Brown.

31 *love-broker,* go-between in love affairs.

36 *curst,* vicious.

37 *witty,* intelligible.

37–8 *invention,* arguments. Possibly there is a quibble on another meaning of invention, something made up, fiction.

38 *licence of ink,* with the freedom that is possible in writing.

*thou thou'st.* To address anyone as 'thou' was a mark of contempt, unless the person concerned was a close friend.

41 *bed of Ware,* a large oaken bedstead capable of holding twelve persons at Ware in Hertfordshire.

42 *gall,* (*a*) gall was an ingredient of ink, (*b*) bitterness, malice.

43 *goose-pen,* (*a*) the normal quill pen, (*b*) the pen belonging to a fool and coward.

45 *cubiculo,* room, chamber. Hotson takes this as a reference to the Cubiculum in Whitehall Palace.

Think out an effective exit for Sir Andrew. Does he go with a quick, jerky stride? Does he come back to enquire where to find them? Does he stand motionless until Sir Toby's 'go'?

46 *manakin,* puppet.

52 *wainropes,* waggon-ropes.

The double gilt of this opportunity you let time wash off, and you are now sailed into the north of my lady's opinion, where you will hang like an icicle on a Dutchman's beard, unless you do redeem it by some laudable attempt either of valour or policy.

SIR ANDREW: An't be any way, it must be with valour, for policy I hate. I had as lief be a Brownist as a politician.

SIR TOBY: Why, then, build me thy fortunes upon the basis of valour. Challenge me the Count's youth to fight with him; hurt him in eleven places. My niece shall take note of it; and assure thyself, there is no love-broker in the world can more prevail in man's commendation with woman than report of valour.

FABIAN: There is no way but this, Sir Andrew.

SIR ANDREW: Will either of you bear me a challenge to him?

SIR TOBY: Go, write it in a martial hand; be curst and brief; it is no matter how witty, so it be eloquent and full of invention. Taunt him with the licence of ink. If thou thou'st him some thrice, it shall not be amiss; and as many lies as will lie in thy sheet of paper, although the sheet were big enough for the bed of Ware in England, set 'em down. Go, about it. Let there be gall enough in thy ink, though thou write with a goose-pen, no matter. About it.

SIR ANDREW: Where shall I find you?

SIR TOBY: We'll call thee at the cubiculo. Go.

[*Exit Sir Andrew*

FABIAN: This is a dear manakin to you, Sir Toby.

SIR TOBY: I have been dear to him, lad—some two thousand strong, or so.

FABIAN: We shall have a rare letter from him. But you'll not deliver't?

SIR TOBY: Never trust me then; and by all means stir on the youth to an answer. I think oxen and wainropes cannot hale them together. For Andrew, if he were opened and you find

55 *anatomy*, corpse.

56–7 *no . . . presage of*, nothing that foretells.

58 *youngest . . . nine*. It was believed that the smallest in a brood of wrens was also the last hatched. A glance at Maria's smallness and perhaps at her name, for the wren was also called Our Lady's hen.

Should Maria enter swiftly and excitedly, or should she enter laughing herself 'into stitches'?

59 *desire . . . spleen*, if you want to burst out laughing.

61 *renegado*, traitor to his faith.

62–3 *impossible . . . grossness*, unbelievable acts of stupidity.

65 *pedant*, schoolmaster.

68 *lines*, rhumb lines. Lines radiating from some sixteen compass points arranged on a circle round a central radiating point on the equator. The lines gave the course of a vessel sailing in any direction continuously.

68–9 *new map . . . Indies*. An allusion to the first map of the world on Mercator's projection, drawn by Edward Wright and published in 1600. In it the 'Indies' were drawn more accurately and augmented by more detail than in previous maps.

Which words fit Sir Toby in this scene: witty, humorous. genial, good-tempered, shabby, cunning, disloyal, sponging, calculating, indifferent, callous, gentlemanly?

## *A Street*

Against Sebastian's wish Antonio has risked the danger of appearing near Orsino's court, and out of his deep friendship has followed Sebastian.

so much blood in his liver as will clog the foot of a flea, I'll eat the rest of th' anatomy.

FABIAN: And his opposite, the youth, bears in his visage no great presage of cruelty.

*Enter* MARIA

SIR TOBY: Look where the youngest wren of nine comes.

MARIA: If you desire the spleen, and will laugh yourselves into stitches, follow me. Yond gull Malvolio is turned heathen, a very renegado; for there is no Christian, that means to be saved by believing rightly, can ever believe such impossible passages of grossness. He's in yellow stockings.

SIR TOBY: And cross-gartered?

MARIA: Most villanously; like a pedant that keeps a school i' th' church. I have dogged him like his murderer. He does obey every point of the letter that I dropped to betray him. He does smile his face into more lines than is in the new map with the augmentation of the Indies. You have not seen such a thing as 'tis. I can hardly forbear hurling things at him. I know my lady will strike him. If she do, he'll smile and take't for a great favour.

SIR TOBY: Come, bring us, bring us where he is.

*Exeunt*

## SCENE THREE

*Enter* SEBASTIAN *and* ANTONIO

SEBASTIAN: I would not by my will have troubled you,
But since you make your pleasure of your pains,
I will no further chide you.

ANTONIO: I could not stay behind you. My desire,

8 *jealousy*, doubt.

9 *skilless*, a stranger, ignorant.

12 *The . . . by*, increased by.

16 *shuffled off*, brushed aside.
*uncurrent*, false, insincere.

19 *relics*, monuments, ancient buildings.
What movement would be suitable here?

28 *it . . . answered*, I could make no defence against such a charge.

34 *traffic's*, trade's.

36 *lapsed*, arrested.

More sharp than filed steel, did spur me forth;
And not all love to see you—though so much
As might have drawn one to a longer voyage—
But jealousy what might befall your travel,
Being skilless in these parts; which to a stranger,
Unguided and unfriended, often prove
Rough and unhospitable. My willing love,
The rather by these arguments of fear,
Set forth in your pursuit.

SEBASTIAN: My kind Antonio,
I can no other answer make but thanks,
And thanks, and ever thanks; and oft good turns
Are shuffled off with such uncurrent pay;
But were my worth as is my conscience firm,
You should find better dealing. What's to do?
Shall we go see the relics of this town?

ANTONIO: To-morrow, sir; best first go see your lodging.

SEBASTIAN: I am not weary, and 'tis long to night.
I pray you let us satisfy our eyes
With the memorials and the things of fame
That do renown this city.

ANTONIO: Would you'd pardon me.
I do not without danger walk these streets.
Once in a sea-fight 'gainst the Count his galleys
I did some service, of such note indeed,
That were I ta'en here, it would scarce be answered.

SEBASTIAN: Belike you slew great number of his people?

ANTONIO: Th' offence is not of such a bloody nature,
Albeit the quality of the time and quarrel
Might well have given us bloody argument.
It might have since been answered in repaying
What we took from them, which, for traffic's sake,
Most of our city did. Only myself stood out.
For which, if I be lapsed in this place,

39 *Elephant*. Shakespeare makes a glance at the Elephant or Oliphant tavern (probably the original of the Elephant and Castle) which was close to the Globe Theatre and apparently frequented by Italians.

44 *toy*, small thing.

45–6 Your own money, I think, is not sufficient to buy luxuries.

What does this deep feeling of Antonio for Sebastian tell us about the latter? (See III. iv. 333–44)

## *Olivia's Garden*

What words describe Olivia's mood: excited, agitated, uncertain, doubtful, fearful, panic-stricken, embarrassed, exhilarated? How does the verse help to suggest her feelings?

3 Young people are more often won over by gifts than by pleading or promising.

Is this spoken to Maria or to herself? If the latter, what can Maria be doing while Olivia is speaking?

5 *sad and civil*, serious and dignified.

9 *possessed*, mad.

Should Maria show any signs of amusement?

I shall pay dear.

SEBASTIAN: Do not then walk too open.

ANTONIO: It doth not fit me. Hold, sir, here's my purse.
In the south suburbs, at the Elephant,
Is best to lodge. I will bespeak our diet,
Whiles you beguile the time and feed your knowledge
With viewing of the town; there shall you have me.

SEBASTIAN: Why I your purse?

ANTONIO: Haply your eye shall light upon some toy
You have desire to purchase; and your store,
I think, is not for idle markets, sir.

SEBASTIAN: I'll be your purse-bearer and leave you for
An hour.

ANTONIO: To th' Elephant.

SEBASTIAN: I do remember.

*Exeunt*

## SCENE FOUR

*Enter* OLIVIA *and* MARIA

OLIVIA: I have sent after him; he says he'll come.
How shall I feast him? What bestow of him?
For youth is bought more oft than begged or borrowed.
I speak too loud.
Where is Malvolio? He is sad and civil,
And suits well for a servant with my fortunes.
Where is Malvolio?

MARIA: He's coming, madam; but in very strange manner. He is sure possessed, madam.

OLIVIA: Why, what's the matter? Does he rave?

MARIA: No, madam, he does nothing but smile. Your lady-

15 This is Malvolio's greatest moment. All his entries can be strikingly effective, but this one, following Maria's preparation of the audience, should be sublimely ludicrous. Think out the possibilities of additional dress or decorations and postures.

17 *Sweet . . . ho.* Malvolio is in ecstasy. How can this be shown in the pitch of his voice?

21 *obstruction in the blood.* Obstruction in the arteries was believed to damage the brain and to lead to fits or madness.

22–23 *true sonnet.* Malvolio is no judge. Probably the 'sonnet' was the ballad:

> 'The crow sits upon the wall,
> Please one and please all'.

26 *Not . . . legs.* There is no melancholy in my mind although my yellow stockings are supposed to signify jealousy.

28 *sweet Roman hand.* The Roman or Italian style of handwriting which (during the sixteenth century) was becoming fashionable. It resembled the present day printer's italic lettering.

29 Olivia feels that the sick Malvolio should be sent to bed.

34 *daws,* jackdaws—noisy birds.

35 *ridiculous boldness.* Marie cunningly chooses words that lead Malvolio to answer by quoting the letter.

37ff. Malvolio applies this to himself with stage business that alarms Olivia.

ship were best to have some guard about you if he come; for sure the man is tainted in's wits.

OLIVIA: Go call him hither. [*Exit Maria*] I am as mad as he,
If sad and merry madness equal be.

*Enter* MARIA *with* MALVOLIO

How now, Malvolio?

MALVOLIO: Sweet lady, ho, ho.

OLIVIA: Smilest thou?
I sent for thee upon a sad occasion. 19

MALVOLIO: Sad, lady! I could be sad. This does make some obstruction in the blood, this cross-gartering; but what of that? If it please the eye of one, it is with me as the very true sonnet is, 'Please one and please all'.

OLIVIA: Why, how dost thou, man? What is the matter with thee?

MALVOLIO: Not black in my mind, though yellow in my legs. It did come to his hands, and commands shall be executed. I think we do know the sweet Roman hand.

OLIVIA: Wilt thou go to bed, Malvolio?

MALVOLIO: To bed? Ay, sweet heart, and I'll come to thee.

OLIVIA: God comfort thee! Why dost thou smile so, and kiss thy hand so oft? 32

MARIA: How do you, Malvolio?

MALVOLIO: At your request? Yes, nightingales answer daws.

MARIA: Why appear you with this ridiculous boldness before my lady?

MALVOLIO: 'Be not afraid of greatness.' 'Twas well writ.

OLIVIA: What meanest thou by that, Malvolio?

MALVOLIO: 'Some are born great'—

OLIVIA: Ha? 40

MALVOLIO: 'Some achieve greatness'—

OLIVIA: What sayest thou?

MALVOLIO: 'And some have greatness thrust upon them.'

50 *made*, (*a*) fortune is made, (*b*) mad.

Olivia does not realize that Malvolio is quoting. Puzzled by the references to yellow stockings and cross-gartering she is completely bewildered by Malvolio's advice that her fortune will be made if she wishes, otherwise she must remain a servant.

61 *come near*, appreciate, understand.

In some productions Malvolio here reclines in lordly manner, after undoing his garters to release the 'obstructions'. On the arrival of Sir Toby, Maria and Fabian he accidentally fastens his garters in such a way as to tie his legs together.

70 *limed her*, caught her as birds used to be caught with gum smeared on reeds or twigs.

71 *fellow*. Normally a contemptuous term, here Malvolio takes it to mean 'companion'.

73 *dram*, a small amount. *scruple*, (*a*) third of a dram, (*b*) doubt.

74 *incredulous*, incredible.

OLIVIA: Heaven restore thee!

MALVOLIO: 'Remember who commended thy yellow stockings'—

OLIVIA: 'Thy yellow stockings'?

MALVOLIO: 'And wished to see thee cross-gartered.'

OLIVIA: 'Cross-gartered'?

MALVOLIO: 'Go to, thou art made, if thou desirest to be so'—

OLIVIA: Am I 'made'?

MALVOLIO: 'If not, let me see thee a servant still.'

OLIVIA: Why, this is very midsummer madness.

*Enter Servant*

SERVANT: Madam, the young gentleman of the Count Orsino's is returned. I could hardly entreat him back. He attends your ladyship's pleasure.

OLIVIA: I'll come to him. [*Exit Servant*]. Good Maria, let this fellow be looked to. Where's my cousin Toby? Let some of my people have a special care of him; I would not have him miscarry for the half of my dowry.

[*Exeunt Olivia and Maria*

MALVOLIO: O, ho, do you come near me now? No worse man than Sir Toby to look to me? This concurs directly with the letter: she sends him on purpose, that I may appear stubborn to him; for she incites me to that in the letter. 'Cast thy humble slough', says she. 'Be opposite with a kinsman, surly with servants; let thy tongue tang with arguments of state; put thyself into the trick of singularity'; and consequently sets down the manner how; as, a sad face, a reverend carriage, a slow tongue, in the habit of some sir of note, and so forth. I have limed her; but it is Jove's doing, and Jove make me thankful. And when she went away now, 'Let this fellow be looked to'. 'Fellow' not 'Malvolio', nor after my degree, but 'fellow'. Why, every thing adheres together, that no dram of a scruple, no scruple of a scruple, no obstacle, no incredulous

78 *in the name of sanctity*. In dealing with devils Sir Toby is taking no chances!

79 *Legion*. A reference to the healing by Our Lord of the man possessed of many devils in the country of the Gadarenes. The unclean spirit said, 'My name is Legion, for we are many', *Mark*, *v*. 9; *Luke*, *viii*. 30.

81–114 This baiting of Malvolio alludes to the symptoms and treatment of madness in Elizabethan times. Maria turns Malvolio's innocent replies into evidence that he is possessed by a devil.

83 *private*, privacy.

85 *how . . . speaks*. Malvolio is being 'opposite' and 'surly' according to the letter. Maria points out that men who were possessed by a devil spoke strangely and roughly as the devil within them spoke with ventriloquistic effect (i.e. speaking hollow).

89 *Let me alone*, leave me to deal with him.

90–1 *defy . . . mankind*, you must not give way to this devil within you. After all the Devil is the Adversary or enemy of all men.

Malvolio is annoyed at Sir Toby's sermonizing tone and the assumption that he is possessed. Maria twists Malvolio's meaning, but before he can take offence adds a remark about Olivia's anxiety for Malvolio.

99 *O Lord!* Is Maria frightened, overcome with laughter, or disgusted?

101 *move him*, upset him.

103 *rough*, violent.

104 *bawcock*, fine fellow.

105–7 *chuck*, *Biddy*. Sir Toby addresses Malvolio as if he were a chicken.

or unsafe circumstance—What can be said? Nothing that can be can come between me and the full prospect of my hopes. Well, Jove, not I, is the doer of this, and he is to be thanked.

*Enter* MARIA *with* SIR TOBY *and* FABIAN

SIR TOBY: Which way is he, in the name of sanctity? If all the devils of hell be drawn in little, and Legion himself possessed him, yet I'll speak to him.

FABIAN: Here he is, here he is. How is't with you, sir?

SIR TOBY: How is't with you, man?

MALVOLIO: Go off, I discard you. Let me enjoy my private. Go off.

MARIA: Lo, how hollow the fiend speaks within him. Did not I tell you? Sir Toby, my lady prays you to have a care of him.

MALVOLIO: Ah ha, does she so?

SIR TOBY: Go to, go to. Peace, peace, we must deal gently with him. Let me alone. How do you, Malvolio? How is't with you? What, man, defy the devil; consider, he's an enemy to mankind.

MALVOLIO: Do you know what you say?

MARIA: La you, an you speak ill of the devil, how he takes it at heart. Pray God, he be not bewitched.

FABIAN: Carry his water to th' wise woman.

MARIA: Marry, and it shall be done tomorrow morning if I live. My lady would not lose him for more than I'll say.

MALVOLIO: How now, mistress?

MARIA: O Lord!

SIR TOBY: Prithee hold thy peace; this is not the way. Do you not see you move him? Let me alone with him.

FABIAN: No way but gentleness; gently, gently. The fiend is rough, and will not be roughly used.

SIR TOBY: Why, how now, my bawcock? How dost thou chuck?

MALVOLIO: Sir!

107–8 A dignified man like you must not play pitch and toss with Satan for your soul.

108 *cherry-pit*. A game in which cherry stones are thrown into a hole. *collier,* coal-miner. The Devil was thought to be black and of course had his professional headquarters in the Pit.

109 *prayers*. Maria sets a neat trap for Malvolio.

114 *element,* world, class.

117–18 This remark reminds the audience that it is 'played on a stage'. Why?

119–20 *His . . . device*. It is his inborn, innermost nature that has caused him to fall a victim to this trick.

121–2 *take . . . taint,* become known and be spoilt.

Which words fit Maria: relentless, vicious, excitable, persistent, cruel, spiteful, irrepressible, playful?

125 *dark . . . bound.* The normal treatment for mad men.

129 *bring . . . bar,* let the practical joke be openly judged.

129–30 *and crown . . . madmen,* acknowledge you the supreme finder of madmen.

The words 'bar', 'crown' and 'finder', however, have a flavour of the law. Perhaps the lines can be freely interpreted, 'We will bring the joke to the bar for judgement and we will make you the coroner (crowner) for the special purpose of giving judgements on madmen!'

131 *More . . . morning,* more fun for May-day games.

134 *saucy*. What is the quibble?

Sir Andrew is well satisfied with his letter. How does he show this while it is being read? Should he mime his own feelings?

SIR TOBY: Ay, Biddy, come with me. What, man, 'tis not for gravity to play at cherry-pit with Satan. Hang him, foul collier!

MARIA: Get him to say his prayers, good Sir Toby, get him to pray.

MALVOLIO: My prayers, minx?

MARIA: No, I warrant you, he will not hear of godliness.

MALVOLIO: Go, hang yourselves all! You are idle shallow things; I am not of your element. You shall know more hereafter. [*Exit*

SIR TOBY: Is't possible?

FABIAN: If this were played upon a stage now, I could condemn it as an improbable fiction.

SIR TOBY: His very genius hath taken the infection of the device, man.

MARIA: Nay, pursue him now, lest the device take air and taint.

FABIAN: Why, we shall make him mad indeed.

MARIA: The house will be the quieter.

SIR TOBY: Come, we'll have him in a dark room and bound. My niece is already in the belief that he's mad. We may carry it thus, for our pleasure and his penance, till our very pastime, tired out of breath, prompt us to have mercy on him; at which time we will bring the device to the bar and crown thee for a finder of madmen. But see, but see.

*Enter* SIR ANDREW

FABIAN: More matter for a May morning.

SIR ANDREW: Here's the challenge, read it. I warrant there's vinegar and pepper in 't.

FABIAN: Is't so saucy?

SIR ANDREW: Ay, is't, I warrant him. Do but read.

SIR TOBY: Give me. [*Reads*] 'Youth, whatsoever thou art, thou art but a scurvy fellow.'

FABIAN: Good and valiant.

139 *admire,* wonder.
Is Fabian ironical or does he congratulate Sir Andrew on avoiding a charge of libel?

152 *windy side,* windward, safe side.

158–9 *in . . . with,* engaged with, busy with.

161 *bum-baily,* a bum-bailiff, an inferior, subordinate sheriff's officer who lay in wait to arrest debtors.

164–5 *gives . . . him,* gains a man more credit for courage than he could obtain by proving it in deeds.

166 Sir Andrew's enthusiasm increases, and he has to be restrained from a practice swear!

172 *clodpole,* blockhead.

SIR TOBY: [*Reads*] 'Wonder not, nor admire not in thy mind, why I do call thee so, for I will show thee no reason for't.'

FABIAN: A good note; that keeps you from the blow of the law.

SIR TOBY: [*Reads*] 'Thou com'st to the Lady Olivia, and in my sight she uses thee kindly; but thou liest in thy throat; that is not the matter I challenge thee for.'

FABIAN: Very brief, and to exceeding good sense—less.

SIR TOBY: [*Reads*] 'I will waylay thee going home; where if it be thy chance to kill me'—

FABIAN: Good.

SIR TOBY: [*Reads*] 'Thou kill'st me like a rogue and a villain.'

FABIAN: Still you keep o' th' windy side of the law. Good.

SIR TOBY: [*Reads*] 'Fare thee well, and God have mercy upon one of our souls! He may have mercy upon mine, but my hope is better, and so look to thyself. Thy friend, as thou usest him, and thy sworn enemy, ANDREW AGUECHEEK.' If this letter move him not, his legs cannot. I'll give't him.

MARIA: You may have very fit occasion for't; he is now in some commerce with my lady, and will by and by depart.

SIR TOBY: Go, Sir Andrew; scout me for him at the corner of the orchard like a bum-baily. So soon as ever thou seest him, draw; and, as thou draw'st, swear horrible; for it comes to pass oft that a terrible oath, with a swaggering accent sharply twanged off, gives manhood more approbation than ever proof itself would have earned him. Away.

SIR ANDREW: Nay, let me alone for swearing. [*Exit*

SIR TOBY: Now will not I deliver his letter; for the behaviour of the young gentleman gives him out to be of good capacity and breeding; his employment between his lord and my niece confirms no less. Therefore this letter, being so excellently ignorant, will breed no terror in the youth; he will find it comes from a clodpole. But, sir, I will deliver his challenge

173–4 *set . . . valour,* describe Aguecheek as having a noteworthy reputation for valour.

177 *cockatrices,* a mythical creature, half serpent and half cockerel, fabled to kill by its glance.

179 *presently,* immediately.

180 *horrid,* hair-raising.

183ff. Olivia reproaches herself for her lack of restraint, yet in the next breath she pleads with Viola and finally utters an outburst of tormented feeling.

183 *And . . . out,* and I have thriftlessly squandered my good name. *out.* Sisson has 'on't', *ie.* Olivia has recklessly made an offering—which has been rejected—as it were on an altar.

189 *jewel,* ornament.

Several movements are needed here. Does Viola accept the jewel?

192–3 *What . . . give,* I will not deny you anything you ask, as long as it may be given without loss of honour.

198 *A fiend like thee.* Devils were supposed to disguise themselves as any person at will. Olivia means that a devil masquerading as Viola would probably destroy her.

by word of mouth; set upon Aguecheek a notable report of valour, and drive the gentleman—as I know his youth will aptly receive it—into a most hideous opinion of his rage, skill, fury and impetuosity. This will so fright them both that they will kill one another by the look, like cockatrices.

*Enter* OLIVIA *with* VIOLA

FABIAN: Here he comes with your niece; give them way till he take leave, and presently after him.

SIR TOBY: I will meditate the while upon some horrid message for a challenge. [*Exeunt Sir Toby, Fabian, and Maria*

OLIVIA: I have said too much unto a heart of stone,
And laid mine honour too unchary out:
There's something in me that reproves my fault;
But such a headstrong potent fault it is,
That it but mocks reproof.

VIOLA: With the same 'haviour that your passion bears
Goes on my master's griefs.

OLIVIA: Here, wear this jewel for me, 'tis my picture.
Refuse it not; it hath no tongue to vex you;
And I beseech you come again tomorrow.
What shall you ask of me that I'll deny,
That honour saved may upon asking give?

VIOLA: Nothing but this—your true love for my master.

OLIVIA: How with mine honour may I give him that
Which I have given to you?

VIOLA: I will acquit you.

OLIVIA: Well, come again to-morrow. Fare thee well.
A fiend like thee might bear my soul to hell. [*Exit*

*Enter* SIR TOBY *and* FABIAN

SIR TOBY: Gentleman, God save thee.

VIOLA: And you, sir.

SIR TOBY: That defence thou hast, betake thee to't. Of what nature the wrongs are thou hast done him, I know not; but

203 *despite,* bitter anger.

204 *Dismount thy tuck,* draw thy sword. *yare,* prompt.

214 *dubbed,* knighted. *unhatched rapier,* a sword not hacked in fight.

215 *on carpet consideration,* kneeling on a carpet, not on the battle-field—a contemptuous phrase for a stay-at-home soldier.

218 *Hob, nob,* hit or miss.

221 *conduct,* escort.

Viola's wit and imagination have enabled her to play the man so far successfully, but this completely unforeseen situation upsets her judgement and confidence. She panics ingloriously at the mere report of Aguecheek's alleged valour.

223 *quirk,* odd behaviour.

Viola makes several attempts to return to the house but Sir Toby and Fabian hold her back.

224–5 *a very competent injury,* a substantial wrong.

229 *meddle,* take part in a fight.

thy intercepter, full of despite, bloody as the hunter, attends thee at the orchard-end. Dismount thy tuck, be yare in thy preparation, for thy assailant is quick, skilful, and deadly.

VIOLA: You mistake, sir, I am sure. No man hath any quarrel to me; my remembrance is very free and clear from any image of offence done to any man.

SIR TOBY: You'll find it otherwise, I assure you. Therefore, if you hold your life at any price, betake you to your guard: for your opposite hath in him what youth, strength, skill and wrath can furnish man withal.

VIOLA: I pray you, sir, what is he?

SIR TOBY: He is knight, dubbed with unhatched rapier and on carpet consideration; but he is a devil in private brawl. Souls and bodies hath he divorced three; and his incensement at this moment is so implacable, that satisfaction can be none but by pangs of death and sepulchre. Hob, nob, is his word; give't or take't.

VIOLA: I will return again into the house and desire some conduct of the lady. I am no fighter. I have heard of some kind of men that put quarrels purposely on others to taste their valour; belike this is a man of that quirk.

SIR TOBY: Sir, no. His indignation derives itself out of a very competent injury; therefore, get you on and give him his desire. Back you shall not to the house, unless you undertake that with me which with as much safety you might answer him. Therefore, on, or strip your sword stark naked; for meddle you must, that's certain, or forswear to wear iron about you.

VIOLA: This is as uncivil as strange. I beseech you do me this courteous office as to know of the knight what my offence to him is. It is something of my negligence, nothing of my purpose.

237 *know,* learn.

239 *mortal arbitrement,* decision by a fight to the death.

243 *opposite,* opponent.

251 *firago,* virago.

Sir Toby possibly pronounces 'firago 'as fire-ago, fire-breather. 'Virago' means a 'heroic maiden', an irony probably not intended by Sir Toby, but which the quick minded Elizabethan courtiers with their delight in word-play would readily detect.

252–3 *stuck in . . . you,* thrust with such deadly swiftness that it cannot be avoided, and on the return he finishes you off.

What are Sir Andrew's reactions in movement and gesture to this description?

257–8 *pacified . . . hold him.* True statements but not in the way Sir Andrew thinks.

What is Viola doing?

263 *motion,* suggestion.

SIR TOBY: I will do so. Signor Fabian, stay you by this gentleman till my return. [*Exit.*

VIOLA: Pray you, sir, do you know of this matter?

FABIAN: I know the knight is incensed against you, even to a mortal arbitrement, but nothing of the circumstance more.

VIOLA: I beseech you, what manner of man is he?

FABIAN: Nothing of that wonderful promise, to read him by his form, as you are like to find him in the proof of his valour. He is indeed, sir, the most skilful, bloody, and fatal opposite that you could possibly have found in any part of Illyria. Will you walk towards him? I will make your peace with him if I can.

VIOLA: I shall be much bound to you for't. I am one that had rather go with sir priest than sir knight. I care not who knows so much of my mettle. [*Exeunt.*

*Enter* SIR TOBY *with* SIR ANDREW

SIR TOBY: Why, man, he's a very devil; I have not seen such a firago. I had a pass with him, rapier, scabbard, and all, and he gives me the stuck in with such a mortal motion, that it is inevitable; and on the answer, he pays you as surely as your feet hit the ground they step on. They say he has been fencer to the Sophy.

SIR ANDREW: Pox on't, I'll not meddle with him.

SIR TOBY: Ay, but he will not now be pacified; Fabian can scarce hold him yonder.

SIR ANDREW: Plague on't, an I thought he had been valiant and so cunning in fence, I'd have seen him damned ere I'd have challenged him. Let him let the matter slip, and I'll give him my horse, grey Capilet.

SIR TOBY: I'll make the motion. Stand here, make a good show on't; this shall end without the perdition of souls [*Aside*] Marry, I'll ride your horse as well as I ride you.

266 *take up,* make up.

268. *He . . . him,* he holds an equally fearful opinion of Sir Andrew.

280 *duello,* the very strict code of honour which governed duelling.

281 *and a soldier.* Should Sir Toby emphasize this?

Try to visualize the duel not as a series of blind cuts and thrusts but with suspense, panics and misdirections. The combatants should place themselves so that Antonio's entry can be an effective surprise and climax to the scene.

291 *undertaker,* one who is spoiling for a fight.

292 Sir Toby and Fabian probably make use of the box-tree again.

*Enter* FABIAN *and* VIOLA

[*To Fabian*] I have his horse to take up the quarrel. I have persuaded him the youth's a devil.

FABIAN: He is as horribly conceited of him; and pants and looks pale, as if a bear were at his heels. 269

SIR TOBY: [*To Viola*] There's no remedy, sir, he will fight with you for's oath sake. Marry, he hath better bethought him of his quarrel, and he finds that now scarce to be worth talking of. Therefore draw for the supportance of his vow, he protests he will not hurt you.

VIOLA: [*Aside*] Pray God defend me. A little thing would make me tell them how much I lack of a man.

FABIAN: Give ground if you see him furious.

SIR TOBY: Come, Sir Andrew, there's no remedy; the gentleman will, for his honour's sake, have one bout with you—he cannot by the duello avoid it—but he has promised me, as he is a gentleman and a soldier, he will not hurt you. Come on; to't. 282

SIR ANDREW: Pray God he keep his oath.

VIOLA: I do assure you 'tis against my will. [*They draw*

*Enter* ANTONIO

ANTONIO: Put up your sword. If this young gentleman
Have done offence, I take the fault on me;
If you offend him, I for him defy you.

SIR TOBY: You, sir? Why, what are you?

ANTONIO: One, sir, that for his love dares yet do more
Than you have heard him brag to you he will. 290

SIR TOBY: Nay, if you be an undertaker, I am for you.
[*They draw*

*Enter Officers*

FABIAN: O good Sir Toby, hold. Here come the officers.

SIR TOBY: I'll be with you anon.

299 *suit,* prosecution brought by.

302 *favour,* face.

311 *You . . . amazed.* What kind of movement or posture will show Viola's amazement?

318 *ability,* extent of my money.

322–3 *Is't . . . persuasion,* is it possible that my previous acts of kindness to you can fail to persuade you to help me?

324 *unsound,* lacking in judgement.

VIOLA: Pray, sir, put your sword up, if you please.

SIR ANDREW: Marry, will I, sir; and, for that I promised you I'll be as good as my word. He will bear you easily and rein, well.

FIRST OFFICER: This is the man; do thy office.

SECOND OFFICER: Antonio, I arrest thee at the suit
Of Count Orsino.

ANTONIO: You do mistake me, sir.

FIRST OFFICER: No, sir, no jot; I know your favour well,
Though now you have no sea-cap on your head.
Take him away; he knows I know him well.

ANTONIO: I must obey. [*To Viola*] This comes with seeking you;
But there's no remedy, I shall answer it.
What will you do, now my necessity
Makes me to ask you for my purse? It grieves me
Much more for what I cannot do for you
Than what befalls myself. You stand amazed,
But be of comfort.

SECOND OFFICER: Come, sir, away.

ANTONIO: I must entreat of you some of that money.

VIOLA: What money, sir?
For the fair kindness you have showed me here,
And part being prompted by your present trouble,
Out of my lean and low ability
I'll lend you something. My having is not much;
I'll make division of my present with you.
Hold, there's half my coffer.

ANTONIO: Will you deny me now?
Is't possible that my deserts to you
Can lack persuasion? Do not tempt my misery,
Lest that it make me so unsound a man
As to upbraid you with those kindnesses
That I have done for you.

331 *O heavens themselves.* Viola's strong words about ingratitude exasperate Antonio who thinks she is not only ungrateful but is impudently hypocritical about it.

336–7 I worshipped what in him seemed to appear of such worth and reverence. Note that Antonio regards Sebastian as god-like (See note I. v, 232).

341–4 In the created world there is no blemish except in men's minds. Only those who are unkind or mis-created are deformed. Goodness is beauty, but beautiful persons with evil minds are soulless bodies whose beauty is the Devil's work.

Viola's ideas about handsome appearances expressed to the Sea Captain earlier on, are now used ironically against her.

Two comments are made on this speech: 'The man grows mad' and 'his words do from such passion fly, That he believes himself'.

How should Antonio deliver his speech to justify these comments?

What is the purpose of the rhyme here (ll. 341–58)?

352–3 *We'll . . . saws,* we can recite couplets containing wise proverbs. A mocking reference to the rhymes just uttered.

354 Oblivious of the others, Viola has moved forward and aside to give her soliloquy.

Which of these words fit Antonio's character: blunt, loyal, frank, courageous, impetuous, rash, impatient, stupid, honest, ill-tempered, adoring?

The rhythm of this long scene is skilfully controlled to bring in four different threads of the plot, ending in the surprising and disconcerting consequences of Viola's disguise both to herself and to Antonio and Sebastian.

VIOLA: I know of none,
Nor know I you by voice or any feature.
I hate ingratitude more in a man
Than lying, vainness, babbling drunkenness,
Or any taint of vice whose strong corruption
Inhabits our frail blood.

ANTONIO: O heavens themselves!

SECOND OFFICER: Come, sir, I pray you, go.

ANTONIO: Let me speak a little. This youth that you see here
I snatched one half out of the jaws of death,
Relieved him with such sanctity of love,
And to his image, which methought did promise
Most venerable worth, did I devotion.

FIRST OFFICER: What's that to us? The time goes by; away.

ANTONIO: But O how vile an idol proves this god.
Thou hast, Sebastian, done good feature shame.
In nature there's no blemish but the mind;
None can be called deformed but the unkind.
Virtue is beauty, but the beauteous evil
Are empty trunks o'erflourished by the devil.

FIRST OFFICER: The man grows mad. Away with him. Come, come, sir.

ANTONIO: Lead me on. [*Exit with Officers*

VIOLA: Methinks his words do from such passion fly,
That he believes himself; so do not I.
Prove true, imagination, O prove true,
That I, dear brother, be now ta'en for you.

SIR TOBY: Come hither, knight; come hither, Fabian. We'll whisper o'er a couplet or two of most sage saws.

VIOLA: He named Sebastian. I my brother know
Yet living in my glass; even such and so
In favour was my brother, and he went
Still in this fashion, colour, ornament,
For him I imitate. O, if it prove,

367 Sir Andrew's courage is rampant, and he departs with brisk ferocity.

Tempests are kind and salt waves fresh in love. [*Exit*

SIR TOBY: A very dishonest paltry boy, and more a coward than a hare: his dishonesty appears in leaving his friend here in necessity and denying him; and for his cowardship, ask Fabian.

FABIAN: A coward, a most devout coward, religious in it.

SIR ANDREW: 'Slid, I'll after him again and beat him.

SIR TOBY: Do; cuff him soundly, but never draw thy sword.

SIR ANDREW: An I do not— [*Exit*

FABIAN: Come, let's see the event.

SIR TOBY: I dare lay any money 'twill be nothing yet.

*Exeunt*

*A Street*

3 *Let . . . thee.* Feste is following Sebastian insisting on giving him Olivia's message for Viola.

4–7 Spoken with emphatic irony.

6–7 *this . . . neither.* Feste perhaps squeezes his nose and speaks nasally.

8 *Vent,* utter. Spoken scornfully.

11–12 *Vent . . . cockney,* I am afraid that this great clumsy world is becoming given over to fanciful speech. To whom is Feste speaking, Sebastian, himself or the audience?

13 *ungird . . . strangeness,* throw off this guise of a stranger. Spoken with mocking sarcasm as a counter to Sebastian's 'vent thy folly'.

15 *Greek,* merry rascal.

What dramatic purpose does this conversation serve?

17 Sebastian turns and moves away from Feste in time to meet Sir Andrew.

18 *hast . . . hand,* art generous.

20 *purchase,* rent, return. The price of land was stated in terms of its annual return, normally it was twelve years' rent. Here Feste means 'at a very high price'.

Should Feste pause after 'report' before adding the rest?

21 What does Sir Andrew do?

25 Sebastian draws his dagger immediately he is attacked by Sir Andrew and is held by Sir Toby. He breaks free from Sir Toby (l. 34) and both he and Sir Toby draw their swords then.

*o'er the house,* (at random) away, into the next street.

# ACT FOUR

## SCENE ONE

*Enter* SEBASTIAN *and* FESTE

FESTE: Will you make me believe that I am not sent for you?

SEBASTIAN: Go to, go to, thou art a foolish fellow.
Let me be clear of thee.

FESTE: Well held out, i' faith. No, I do not know you; nor I am not sent to you by my lady, to bid you come speak with her; nor your name is not Master Cesario; nor this is not my nose neither. Nothing that is so, is so.

SEBASTIAN: I prithee vent thy folly somewhere else.
Thou know'st not me.

FESTE: Vent my folly! He has heard that word of some great man and now applies it to a fool. Vent my folly! I am afraid this great lubber, the world, will prove a cockney. I prithee now, ungird thy strangeness, and tell me what I shall vent to my lady. Shall I vent to her that thou art coming?

SEBASTIAN: I prithee, foolish Greek, depart from me;
There's money for thee. If you tarry longer,
I shall give worse payment.

FESTE: By my troth, thou hast an open hand. These wise men that give fools money get themselves a good report, after fourteen years' purchase.

*Enter* SIR ANDREW, SIR TOBY, *and* FABIAN

SIR ANDREW: Now, sir, have I met you again? There's for you.

SEBASTIAN: Why, there's for thee, and there, and there.
Are all the people mad?

SIR TOBY: Hold, sir, or I'll throw your dagger o'er the house.

34–5 *young . . . iron.* To whom is Sir Toby speaking, Sebastian or Sir Andrew?

35 *you . . . fleshed,* you have had enough fighting to begin with.

39 *malapert,* saucy, impertinent.

40 *Hold . . . hold.* With what movement and gesture does Olivia intervene?

41 *Madam!* With what movement and gesture does Sir Toby greet Olivia?

46 *Rudesby,* rough, insolent fellow.
Is Sir Toby about to protest so that Olivia turns on him again?

48 *extent,* attack.

53 *Beshrew,* confound.

54 *started,* startled.
*heart . . . thee,* the heart that I have already given you (i.e. Viola).

55 *What . . . this?* What does this mean? What suggestion is this?

FESTE: This will I tell my lady straight. I would not be in some of your coats for twopence. [*Exit*

SIR TOBY: Come on, sir; hold.

SIR ANDREW: Nay, let him alone: I'll go another way to work with him. I'll have an action of battery against him, if there be any law in Illyria. Though I struck him first, yet it's no matter for that.

SEBASTIAN: Let go thy hand.

SIR TOBY: Come, sir, I will not let you go. Come, my young soldier, put up your iron; you are well fleshed. Come on.

SEBASTIAN: I will be free from thee. What wouldst thou now?
If thou darest tempt me further, draw thy sword. [*Draws*

SIR TOBY: What, what? Nay, then I must have an ounce or two of this malapert blood from you. [*Draws*

*Enter* OLIVIA

OLIVIA: Hold, Toby; on thy life I charge thee hold.

SIR TOBY: Madam!

OLIVIA: Will it be ever thus? Ungracious wretch,
Fit for the mountains and the barbarous caves,
Where manners ne'er were preached. Out of my sight!
Be not offended, dear Cesario.
Rudesby, be gone! [*Exeunt Sir Toby, Sir Andrew, and Fabian*
I prithee, gentle friend,
Let thy fair wisdom, not thy passion, sway
In this uncivil and unjust extent
Against thy peace. Go with me to my house,
And hear thou there how many fruitless pranks
This ruffian hath botched up, that thou thereby
Mayst smile at this. Thou shalt not choose but go;
Do not deny. Beshrew his soul for me,
He started one poor heart of mine in thee.

SEBASTIAN: What relish is in this? How runs the stream?
Or I am mad, or else this is a dream.

57 *Lethe*. In classical legend one of the rivers of the underworld whose waters brought forgetfulness.

57–8 Let my fancy keep my common sense drowned in oblivion. If this delicious experience is a dream may I go on sleeping.

What is Olivia doing while Sebastian says these lines?

59 How does Olivia lead Sebastian off?

Is it Olivia's beauty and attractiveness that make Sebastian forget to admit that he is not Cesario?

What words fit his character: plain, downright, bemused, natural, fresh, practical, opportunist, muddled, easily-led?

## *Olivia's House*

Where on an Elizabethan stage would Malvolio be imprisoned?

1 *Nay, I prithee.* Is Feste reluctant to disguise himself as a parson?

2 *Sir,* the usual title of a clergyman.

*Topas,* probably a glance at the Elizabethan belief that the jewel topaz cured madness.

5 *would . . . dissembled.* See I. v, 49–50.

9 *competitors,* fellow conspirators.

11 Feste uses parson-like tones.

11, 13 The old hermit of Prague and the niece of King Gorboduc are flights of Feste's fancy. *Gorboduc,* however, was a play well known to Shakespeare's audience about a mythical British king.

17 *Peace in.* The normal greeting of a priest on visiting a house.

Let fancy still my sense in Lethe steep;
If it be thus to dream, still let me sleep.

OLIVIA: Nay, come, I prithee. Would thou'dst be ruled by me.

SEBASTIAN: Madam, I will.

OLIVIA: O say so, and so be.

*Exeunt*

## SCENE TWO

*Enter* MARIA *and* FESTE

MARIA: Nay, I prithee put on this gown and this beard; make him believe thou art Sir Topas the curate; do it quickly. I'll call Sir Toby the whilst. [*Exit*

FESTE: Well, I'll put it on, and I will dissemble myself in't; and would I were the first that ever dissembled in such a gown. I am not tall enough to become the function well, nor lean enough to be thought a good student; but to be said an honest man and a good housekeeper goes as fairly as to say a careful man and a great scholar. The competitors enter.

*Enter* SIR TOBY *and* MARIA

SIR TOBY: Jove bless thee, master Parson.

FESTE: Bonos dies, Sir Toby: for as the old hermit of Prague, that never saw pen and ink, very wittily said to a niece of King Gorboduc, 'That that is, is': so I, being master Parson, am master Parson; for, what is 'that', but 'that'; and 'is', but 'is'?

SIR TOBY: To him, Sir Topas.

FESTE: What ho, I say. Peace in this prison.

18 In what way besides using certain words and wearing a cloak and beard does Feste imitate a parson?

24 *hyperbolical.* A diabolical fiend would be normal, Feste uses hyperbolical to suggest a far worse fiend if it causes Malvolio to rave about women.

Remember here and 'Satan' (l. 30) that Feste assumes that it is the devil possessing Malvolio who is speaking ventriloquially.

35 *barricadoes,* barricades.

36 *clerestories,* small windows above the arches in a church or high up in the hall of a mansion. Hotson sees a reference here to the Great Hall in the palace of Whitehall.

37 *obstruction,* i.e. to the view. Malvolio had of course complained earlier about 'obstruction' in the blood.

40–1 *no . . . ignorance.* Possibly a glance at the Scriptures. (See *Ephesians,* iv. 18).

41–2 *Egyptians . . . fog. Exodus,* x. 22–3.

46 *constant question,* properly ordered discussion.

47 *Pythagoras,* a Greek philosopher, who taught that the souls of human beings passed after death into animals.

SIR TOBY: The knave counterfeits well; a good knave.

MALVOLIO: [*Within*] Who calls there?

FESTE: Sir Topas the curate, who comes to visit Malvolio the lunatic.

MALVOLIO: Sir Topas, Sir Topas, good Sir Topas, go to my lady.

FESTE: Out, hyperbolical fiend! How vexest thou this man. Talkest thou nothing but of ladies?

SIR TOBY: Well said, Master Parson.

MALVOLIO: Sir Topas, never was man thus wronged. Good Sir Topas, do not think I am mad; they have laid me here in hideous darkness.

FESTE: Fie, thou dishonest Satan! I call thee by the most modest terms, for I am one of those gentle ones that will use the devil himself with courtesy. Sayest thou that house is dark?

MALVOLIO: As hell, Sir Topas.

FESTE: Why, it hath bay windows transparent as barricadoes, and the clerestories toward the south north are as lustrous as ebony; and yet complainest thou of obstruction?

MALVOLIO: I am not mad, Sir Topas; I say to you this house is dark.

FESTE: Madman, thou errest. I say there is no darkness but ignorance, in which thou art more puzzled than the Egyptians in their fog.

MALVOLIO: I say this house is dark as ignorance, though ignorance were as dark as hell; and I say, there was never man thus abused. I am no more mad than you are; make the trial of it in any constant question.

FESTE: What is the opinion of Pythagoras concerning wild fowl?

MALVOLIO: That the soul of our grandam might haply inhabit a bird.

FESTE: What thinkest thou of his opinion?

55–6 *allow . . . wits,* admit that you are sane.

56 *woodcock,* a bird believed not to have any wit.

60 *for all waters,* I can assume any quality you like. Possibly a reference to the 'waters' of a jewel (topaz).

61–2 Maria's comment probably leads Sir Toby to seek a way out from a prank which he realizes has gone far enough.

64–8 *I would . . . chamber.* Is this spoken to Maria alone?

65 *conveniently delivered,* quietly freed.

68 Should Feste have a pipe and tabor intermezzo here before he sings?

69 *Hey, Robin.* See Appendix III.

82 *fell . . . wits,* lost your reason.

MALVOLIO: I think nobly of the soul, and no way approve his opinion.

FESTE: Fare thee well. Remain thou still in darkness. Thou shalt hold the opinion of Pythagoras ere I will allow of thy wits, and fear to kill a woodcock, lest thou dispossess the soul of thy grandam. Fare thee well.

MALVOLIO: Sir Topas, Sir Topas—

SIR TOBY: My most exquisite Sir Topas.

FESTE: Nay, I am for all waters.

MARIA: Thou mightst have done this without thy beard and gown; he sees thee not.

SIR TOBY: To him in thine own voice, and bring me word how thou find'st him. I would we were well rid of this knavery. If he may be conveniently delivered, I would he were; for I am now so far in offence with my niece that I cannot pursue with any safety this sport to the upshot. Come by and by to my chamber.

[*Exeunt Sir Toby and Maria*

FESTE: [*Sings*] 'Hey, Robin, jolly Robin,
Tell me how thy lady does.'

MALVOLIO: Fool!

FESTE: [*Sings*] 'My lady is unkind, perdy.'

MALVOLIO: Fool!

FESTE: [*Sings*] 'Alas, why is she so?'

MALVOLIO: Fool, I say!

FESTE: [*Sings*] 'She loves another'—Who calls, ha?

MALVOLIO: Good fool, as ever thou wilt deserve well at my hand, help me to a candle, and pen, ink, and paper. As I am a gentleman, I will live to be thankful to thee for't.

FESTE: Master Malvolio?

MALVOLIO: Ay, good fool.

FESTE: Alas, sir, how fell you besides your five wits?

MALVOLIO: Fool, there was never man so notoriously abused. I am as well in my wits, fool, as thou art.

87 *propertied,* made a tool of.

91ff. *Malvolio . . .* In the following conversation Feste rapidly alters his position as well as his voice.

92 *vain bibble-babble.* I *Timothy,* vi. 20; II *Timothy,* ii. 16.

98 *shent,* blamed.

113 *I am gone, sir.* See Appendix III.

117 *Vice,* a comic character in the medieval morality plays. He usually wore a long wooden dagger with which he belaboured another character representing the Devil and whose talons he tried to cut.

FESTE: But as well? Then you are mad indeed, if you be no better in your wits than a fool.

MALVOLIO: They have here propertied me; keep me in darkness, send ministers to me, asses, and do all they can to face me out of my wits.

FESTE: Advise you what you say; the minister is here. Malvolio, Malvolio, thy wits the heavens restore. Endeavour thyself to sleep, and leave thy vain bibble babble.

MALVOLIO: Sir Topas—

FESTE: Maintain no words with him, good fellow. Who, I, sir? not I, sir. God be wi' you, good Sir Topas. Marry, amen. I will, sir, I will.

MALVOLIO: Fool, fool, fool, I say—

FESTE: Alas, sir, be patient. What say you, sir? I am shent for speaking to you.

MALVOLIO: Good fool, help me to some light and some paper. I tell thee, I am as well in my wits as any man in Illyria.

FESTE: Well-a-day that you were, sir!

MALVOLIO: By this hand, I am. Good fool, some ink, paper and light; and convey what I will set down to my lady. It shall advantage thee more than ever the bearing of letter did.

FESTE: I will help you to't. But tell me true, are you not mad indeed, or do you but counterfeit?

MALVOLIO: Believe me, I am not. I tell thee true.

FESTE: Nay, I'll ne'er believe a madman till I see his brains. I will fetch you light and paper and ink.

MALVOLIO: Fool, I'll requite it in the highest degree. I prithee be gone.

FESTE: [*Sings*] I am gone, sir,
And anon, sir,
I'll be with you again,
In a trice,
Like to the old Vice,
Your need to sustain;

119 Feste may give a burlesque of the Vice's activities at this point by pretending to drive away Malvolio's devil.

Which words fit Feste: sympathetic, merciless, callous, a turncoat, venal, frivolous?

## *Olivia's Garden*

Sebastian is still bewildered. What actions are implied in ll. 1 and 2?

6 *credit*, general opinion.

9–10 For although my innermost feelings argue strongly against my impression of madness in this affair, and persuade me that this may be some mistake . . . .

11 *accident*, event. *flood*, high tide.

12 *instance*, example. *discourse*, reason

15 *trust*, belief.

Who with dagger of lath,
In his rage and his wrath,
  Cries, Ah ha, to the devil;
Like a mad lad,
Pare thy nails, dad.
  Adieu, goodman devil. [*Exit*

## SCENE THREE

*Enter* SEBASTIAN

SEBASTIAN: This is the air; that is the glorious sun;
This pearl she gave me, I do feel't and see't.
And though 'tis wonder that enwraps me thus,
Yet 'tis not madness. Where's Antonio, then?
I could not find him at the Elephant,
Yet there he was; and there I found this credit,
That he did range the town to seek me out.
His counsel now might do me golden service;
For though my soul disputes well with my sense
That this may be some error, but no madness,
Yet doth this accident and flood of fortune
So far exceed all instance, all discourse,
That I am ready to distrust mine eyes
And wrangle with my reason that persuades me
To any other trust but that I am mad,
Or else the lady's mad. Yet, if 'twere so,
She could not sway her house, command her followers,
Take and give back affairs and their dispatch
With such a smooth, discreet, and stable bearing
As I perceive she does. There's something in't
That is deceivable. But here the lady comes.

24 *chantry*, private chapel.

26 The ceremony is a betrothal, not a wedding. It was probably almost equivalent to a civil marriage.

29 *Whiles*, until.

30 *What time*, at that time.
What is the dramatic value of concealing the betrothal?

35 *fairly note*, favourably regard, clearly grace.
Olivia and Sebastian are going to their betrothal—practically the equivalent of a marriage. It is a rapturous and solemn moment, and their exit must convey the dignity and intensity of the situation. How will they walk—slowly, quickly, abreast, in line astern, in step? Where will they look—at the priest, at each other, on the ground? Will their hands be at their sides, linked, raised, clasped, at each other's waists?

## *Act Four, Scene Three*

*Enter* OLIVIA *and Priest*

OLIVIA: Blame not this haste of mine. If you mean well,
Now go with me and with this holy man
Into the chantry by. There, before him,
And underneath that consecrated roof,
Plight me the full assurance of your faith,
That my most jealous and too doubtful soul
May live at peace. He shall conceal it
Whiles you are willing it shall come to note,
What time we will our celebration keep
According to my birth. What do you say?

SEBASTIAN: I'll follow this good man, and go with you;
And, having sworn truth, ever will be true.

OLIVIA: Then lead the way, good father; and heavens so shine
That they may fairly note this act of mine.

*Exeunt*

*A Street*

Twice in this scene the Viola-Sebastian tangle is about to be cleared, but Shakespeare increases suspense by interruptions until Sebastian himself appears.

1–6 What stage business between Feste and Fabian would be suitable?

1 *letter,* i.e. Malvolio's letter.

2 *another,* i.e. in exchange.

5–6 Probably a topical joke referring to Dr. Bullein and Queen Elizabeth I. 'Shee demaunded his dogge; he gave it. "Nowe Madame", quoth he, "you promised to give me my desyre". "I will", quoth she. "Then I pray you give me my dog againe."'

6 The grouping of characters and their entries demands some thought. All the characters except Maria appear during this scene.

18 *conclusions,* logical conclusions.

18–19 *four negatives,* 'four lips' which are opposite or opposed, i.e. negative, but they make two consenting (affirming) mouths in contact.

Another explanation is that when a lady says, 'No, no', she means, 'Yes'.

22–3 *though . . . friends.* What is the hint?

# ACT FIVE

## SCENE ONE

*Enter* FESTE *and* FABIAN

FABIAN: Now, as thou lovest me, let me see his letter.

FESTE: Good Master Fabian, grant me another request.

FABIAN: Any thing.

FESTE: Do not desire to see this letter.

FABIAN: This is to give a dog, and in recompense desire my dog again.

*Enter* DUKE, VIOLA, CURIO, *and Lords*

DUKE: Belong you to the Lady Olivia, friends?

FESTE: Ay, sir, we are some of her trappings.

DUKE: I know thee well. How dost thou, my good fellow?

FESTE: Truly, sir, the better for my foes and the worse for my friends.

DUKE: Just the contrary: the better for thy friends.

FESTE: No, sir, the worse.

DUKE: How can that be?

FESTE: Marry, sir, they praise me and make an ass of me. Now my foes tell me plainly I am an ass; so that by my foes, sir, I profit in the knowledge of myself, and by my friends I am abused; so that, conclusions to be as kisses, if your four negatives make your two affirmatives, why then, the worse for my friends and the better for my foes.

DUKE: Why, this is excellent.

FESTE: By my troth, sir, no; though it please you to be one of my friends.

DUKE: Thou shalt not be the worse for me—there's gold.

28 *Put . . . pocket,* (*a*) put your Grace's hand in your pocket, (*b*) put away your virtue.

29 *obey it,* i.e. ill-counsel to be a double-dealer.

32 *Primo . . . tertio.* A game of chance, perhaps with dice.

33 *triplex,* three time in music.

34 *tripping,* (*a*) dancing, (*b*) a quibble on 'trip' in the game 'trey trip' in which the aim was to throw a three at dice.
*bells . . . Bennet.* This may be a reference to a song now lost, or to one of the St. Bennet churches in the city of London.

36 *throw.* The Duke laughingly follows up the reference to dicing with a pun, (*a*) occasion, (*b*) throw of dice.

What is the dramatic value of this episode (ll. 7-43)? Is it to give further information about the Duke's character, to give comic relief, to suggest the passage of time, or to heighten suspense?

47 *Vulcan.* In Roman mythology the god of fire and metal-working.

48 *baubling,* small.

49 *unprizable,* worthless.

50 *scathful grapple,* damaging attack.

51 *bottom,* ship.

52 *That . . . loss,* that even those at enmity with him and who had suffered loss at his hands.

55 *fraught,* cargo. *Candy,* Crete.

FESTE: But that it would be double-dealing, sir, I would you could make it another.

DUKE: O, you give me ill counsel.

FESTE: Put your grace in your pocket, sir, for this once, and let your flesh and blood obey it.

DUKE: Well, I will be so much a sinner to be a double-dealer: there's another.

FESTE: Primo, secundo, tertio, is a good play; and the old saying is 'The third pays for all'. The triplex, sir, is a good tripping measure; or the bells of Saint Bennet, sir, may put you in mind—one, two, three.

DUKE: You can fool no more money out of me at this throw. If you will let your lady know I am here to speak with her, and bring her along with you, it may awake my bounty further.

FESTE: Marry, sir, lullaby to your bounty till I come again. I go, sir; but I would not have you to think that my desire of having is the sin of covetousness. But, as you say, sir, let your bounty take a nap, I will awake it anon. [*Exit*

*Enter* ANTONIO *and Officers*

VIOLA: Here comes the man, sir, that did rescue me.

DUKE: That face of his I do remember well;
Yet when I saw it last, it was besmeared
As black as Vulcan in the smoke of war.
A baubling vessel was he captain of,
For shallow draught and bulk unprizable,
With which such scathful grapple did he make
With the most noble bottom of our fleet,
That very envy and the tongue of loss
Cried fame and honour on him. What's the matter?

FIRST OFFICER: Orsino, this is that Antonio
That took the Phoenix and her fraught from Candy;
And this is he that did the Tiger board,

58 *desperate . . . state,* showing no shame for his own crimes nor care for the good order of the state.

62 *but distraction,* unless it were madness.

65 *dear,* dire, grievous.

73 *wreck,* shipwrecked person.

88 *Three months.* It is apparently three days. Does three months 'feel' about right for what has happened earlier in the play?

When your young nephew Titus lost his leg.
Here in the streets, desperate of shame and state,
In private brabble did we apprehend him.

VIOLA: He did me kindness, sir, drew on my side;
But in conclusion put strange speech upon me.
I know not what 'twas but distraction.

DUKE: Notable pirate, thou salt-water thief,
What foolish boldness brought thee to their mercies,
Whom thou, in terms so bloody and so dear,
Hast made thine enemies?

ANTONIO: Orsino, noble sir,
Be pleased that I shake off these names you give me:
Antonio never yet was thief or pirate,
Though I confess, on base and ground enough,
Orsino's enemy. A witchcraft drew me hither.
That most ingrateful boy there by your side,
From the rude sea's enraged and foamy mouth
Did I redeem; a wreck past hope he was.
His life I gave him, and did thereto add
My love without retention or restraint,
All his in dedication. For his sake
Did I expose myself, pure for his love,
Into the danger of this adverse town;
Drew to defend him when he was beset:
Where being apprehended, his false cunning,
Not meaning to partake with me in danger,
Taught him to face me out of his acquaintance,
And grew a twenty years removed thing
While one would wink; denied me mine own purse,
Which I had recommended to his use
Not half an hour before.

VIOLA: How can this be?

DUKE: When came he to this town?

ANTONIO: Today, my lord; and for three months before,

97 Olivia has moved to Viola.

100 *Good my lord.* Olivia turns from the Duke to hear Viola. Any gesture or movement required from them?

103 *fat . . . fulsome,* offensive and distasteful.

106 *uncivil.* Has Olivia been discourteous?

112 *Egyptian thief.* A reference to an episode in a Greek novel which had been translated into English in 1569. The lovers Meagenes and Chariclea were captured by Thyamis ('the Egyptian thief') who fell in love with Chariclea. Surrounded by his enemies, Thyamis determined to kill Chariclea, but in the darkness killed another person and Chariclea escaped.

117 *screws,* wrenches.

No interim, not a minute's vacancy,
Both day and night did we keep company.

*Enter* OLIVIA *and Attendants*

DUKE: Here comes the Countess: now heaven walks on earth.
But for thee, fellow—fellow, thy words are madness—
Three months this youth hath tended upon me;
But more of that anon. Take him aside.

OLIVIA: What would my lord, but that he may not have,
Wherein Olivia may seem serviceable?
Cesario, you do not keep promise with me.

VIOLA: Madam?

DUKE: Gracious Olivia—

OLIVIA: What do you say, Cesario? Good my lord—

VIOLA: My lord would speak; my duty hushes me.

OLIVIA: If it be aught to the old tune, my lord,
It is as fat and fulsome to mine ear
As howling after music.

DUKE: Still so cruel?

OLIVIA: Still so constant, lord.

DUKE: What, to perverseness? You uncivil lady,
To whose ingrate and unauspicious altars
My soul the faithfull'st offerings hath breathed out
That e'er devotion tendered. What shall I do?

OLIVIA: Even what is please my lord, that shall become him.

DUKE: Why should I not, had I the heart to do it,
Like to th' Egyptian thief at point of death,
Kill what I love?—a savage jealousy
That sometime savours nobly. But hear me this:
Since you to non-regardance cast my faith,
And that I partly know the instrument
That screws me from my true place in your favour,
Live you the marble-breasted tyrant still.

119 *minion,* darling.

121–2 *Him . . . crowned.* A reference to a belief that the triumphant (crowned) lover is mirrored as in a crystal in his lady's eyes.

119–25 What gestures and movements are required here?

The Duke's mood has changed from good humour at the beginning of the scene, through a somewhat hostile attitude towards Antonio, to a jealous rage.

127 *do . . . rest,* give you peace of mind.

133 *detested,* (*a*) hated, (*b*) renounced on oath.

137 *husband.* Anguish forces Olivia to reveal what she had promised to hide.

139 Is the audience intended to laugh at this or to take it seriously?

141 *strangle . . . propriety,* suppress your own true state.

144 *that . . . fear'st,* i.e. the Duke.

But this your minion, whom I know you love,
And whom, by heaven I swear, I tender dearly,
Him will I tear out of that cruel eye
Where he sits crowned in his master's spite.
Come, boy, with me; my thoughts are ripe in mischief.
I'll sacrifice the lamb that I do love,
To spite a raven's heart within a dove.
VIOLA: And I, most jocund, apt, and willingly,
To do you rest, a thousand deaths would die.
OLIVIA: Where goes Cesario?
VIOLA: After him I love
More than I love these eyes, more than my life,
More, by all mores, than e'er I shall love wife.
If I do feign, you witnesses above
Punish my life for tainting of my love.
OLIVIA: Ay me detested, how am I beguiled!
VIOLA: Who does beguile you? Who does do you wrong?
OLIVIA: Hast thou forgot thyself? Is it so long?
Call forth the holy father. [*Exit Attendant*
DUKE: Come, away!
OLIVIA: Whither, my lord? Cesario, husband, stay.
DUKE: Husband?
OLIVIA: Ay, husband: can he that deny?
DUKE: Her husband, sirrah?
VIOLA: No, my lord, not I.
OLIVIA: Alas, it is the baseness of thy fear
That makes thee strangle thy propriety.
Fear not, Cesario, take thy fortunes up;
Be that thou know'st thou art, and then thou art
As great as that thou fear'st.

*Enter Priest*

O, welcome, father!
Father, I charge thee, by thy reverence,

155 *function,* office as priest.
The priest's detailed speech shows that no part of the ceremony was omitted, the contract was confirmed, attested, strengthened and sealed.

158–9 O deceitful young fox that you are now, what will you be like when that fox skin of yours has grey hairs in it?

161 *trip,* (*a*) trap, (*b*) throw (in wrestling).

164 Was Viola going to admit her disguise?
*swear,* i.e. an oath.

165 *little,* a little.
How should Olivia say this, bitterly, jestingly, laughingly, tauntingly, jeeringly, sadly?

166 A very effective relaxing of the tension and frustration caused by the recriminations. Sir Andrew's entry and shout should be carefully timed. Should the one precede the other? The few moments of farcical comedy bring in Sebastian and lead straight to the resolving of the situation.
Does anyone go to assist Sir Andrew?

167 *presently,* immediately.

170 *coxcomb,* head.

174 *incardinate,* incarnate, in the flesh. Sir Andrew's gift for languages again!

176 *'Od's lifelings . . . is!* How will Sir Andrew show his sudden fright?

Here to unfold—though lately we intended
To keep in darkness what occasion now
Reveals before 'tis ripe—what thou dost know
Hath newly passed between this youth and me.

PRIEST: A contract of eternal bond of love,
Confirmed by mutual joinder of your hands,
Attested by the holy close of lips,
Strengthened by interchangement of your rings;
And all the ceremony of this compact
Sealed in my function, by my testimony;
Since when, my watch hath told me, toward my grave
I have travelled but two hours.

DUKE: O thou dissembling cub! What wilt thou be
When time hath sowed a grizzle on thy case?
Or will not else thy craft so quickly grow,
That thine own trip shall be thine overthrow?
Farewell, and take her; but direct thy feet
Where thou and I henceforth may never meet.

VIOLA: My lord, I do protest—

OLIVIA: O, do not swear!
Hold little faith, though thou hast too much fear.

*Enter* SIR ANDREW

SIR ANDREW: For the love of God, a surgeon!
Send one presently to Sir Toby.

OLIVIA: What's the matter?

SIR ANDREW: He has broke my head across, and has given Sir Toby a bloody coxcomb too. For the love of God, your help! I had rather than forty pound I were at home.

OLIVIA: Who has done this, Sir Andrew?

SIR ANDREW: The Count's gentleman, one Cesario. We took him for a coward, but he's the very devil incardinate.

DUKE: My gentleman, Cesario?

SIR ANDREW: 'Od's lifelings, here he is! You broke my head

183 *set nothing by,* think nothing of.

184 *halting,* staggering.

185 *tickled,* i.e. with his rapier.

189 *sot,* fool.

191 *set,* closed, fixed and glassy.

192 *passy measures pavin.* An English form of the Italian passemezzo pavana, a kind of pavane, or slow dance. Sir Toby plays on Feste's 'set at eight' for the point of the remark is that this pavane was set to a number of rhythmical sections of eight bars each.

200 The grouping and positioning of characters needs care to bring out the depth of feeling in this meeting of the twins. Sebastian has eyes only for Olivia, how is his attention attracted to Antonio?

Should Sebastian see Viola immediately, or should he turn to her as Antonio speaks?

202 *wit . . . safety,* out of consideration for my safety.

for nothing; and that that I did, I was set on to do't by Sir Toby.

VIOLA: Why do you speak to me? I never hurt you.
You drew your sword upon me without cause,
But I bespake you fair, and hurt you not.

*Enter* SIR TOBY *and* FESTE

SIR ANDREW: If a bloody coxcomb be a hurt, you have hurt me; I think you set nothing by a bloody coxcomb.
Here comes Sir Toby halting; you shall hear more: but if he had not been in drink, he would have tickled you othergates than he did.

DUKE: How now, gentleman? How is't with you?

SIR TOBY: That's all one; has hurt me, and there's the end on't. Sot, didst see Dick surgeon, sot?

FESTE: O, he's drunk, Sir Toby, an hour agone; his eyes were set at eight i' th' morning.

SIR TOBY: Then he's a rogue: and a passy measures pavin. I hate a drunken rogue.

OLIVIA: Away with him. Who hath made this havoc with them?

SIR ANDREW: I'll help you, Sir Toby, because we'll be dressed together.

SIR TOBY: Will you help—an ass-head and a coxcomb and a knave, a thin-faced knave, a gull?

OLIVIA: Get him to bed, and let his hurt be looked to.

[*Exeunt Feste, Fabian, Sir Toby, and Sir Andrew*

*Enter* SEBASTIAN

SEBASTIAN: I am sorry, madam, I have hurt your kinsman;
But, had it been the brother of my blood,
I must have done no less with wit and safety.
You throw a strange regard upon me, and by that
I do perceive it hath offended you.
Pardon me, sweet one, even for the vows

207 *habit,* dress.

208 *a . . . perspective,* an optical illusion in real life.

218–19 *Nor . . . where,* I am not a god that I can be present in more than one place at one time.

225 *So . . . suited,* dressed as you are.
It was common belief that devils could appear to anyone in the shape of a friend recently dead. Hence Viola is anxious and cautious.

228 *dimension . . . clad,* clothed in an earthly body.

229 *participate,* inherit.

230 *goes even,* fits in.

We made each other but so late ago.
DUKE: One face, one voice, one habit, and two persons.
A natural perspective, that is and is not.
SEBASTIAN: Antonio, O my dear Antonio!
How have the hours racked and tortured me,
Since I have lost thee!
ANTONIO: Sebastian are you?
SEBASTIAN: Fear'st thou that, Antonio?
ANTONIO: How have you made division of yourself?
An apple, cleft in two, is not more twin
Than these two creatures. Which is Sebastian?
OLIVIA: Most wonderful.
SEBASTIAN: Do I stand there? I never had a brother;
Nor can there be that deity in my nature,
Of here and everywhere. I had a sister,
Whom the blind waves and surges have devoured.
Of charity, what kin are you to me?
What countryman? What name? What parentage?
VIOLA: Of Messaline; Sebastian was my father,
Such a Sebastian was my brother too,
So went he suited to his watery tomb.
If spirits can assume both form and suit
You come to fright us.
SEBASTIAN: A spirit I am indeed,
But am in that dimension grossly clad
Which from the womb I did participate.
Were you a woman, as the rest goes even,
I should my tears let fall upon your cheek,
And say 'Thrice welcome, drowned Viola'.
VIOLA: My father had a mole upon his brow.
SEBASTIAN: And so had mine.
VIOLA: And died that day when Viola from her birth
Had numbered thirteen years.
SEBASTIAN: O, that record is lively in my soul.

240 *lets,* hinders.

243 *jump,* agree.

251 *But nature . . . that,* but nature led you truly even in that.

256 *the glass . . . true,* these apparent reflections (Viola and Sebastian) are real people.

262 *orbed continent,* the heavens.

266 *action,* law suit.

267 *durance,* prison. *suit,* instigation.

He finished indeed his mortal act
That day that made my sister thirteen years.
VIOLA: If nothing lets to make us happy both
But this my masculine usurped attire,
Do not embrace me till each circumstance
Of place, time, fortune, do cohere and jump
That I am Viola; which to confirm,
I'll bring you to a captain in this town,
Where lie my maiden weeds; by whose gentle help
I was preserved to serve this noble Count.
All the occurrence of my fortune since
Hath been between this lady and this lord.
SEBASTIAN: [*To Olivia*] So comes it, lady, you have been mistook;
But nature to her bias drew in that.
You would have been contracted to a maid;
Nor are you therein, by my life, deceived,
You are betrothed both to a maid and man.
DUKE: Be not amazed, right noble is his blood.
If this be so, as yet the glass seems true,
I shall have share in this most happy wreck.
[*To Viola*] Boy, thou hast said to me a thousand times
Thou never shouldst love woman like to me.
VIOLA: And all these sayings will I over-swear;
And all those swearings keep as true in soul
As doth that orbed continent the fire
That severs day from night.
DUKE: Give me thy hand,
And let me see thee in thy woman's weeds.
VIOLA: The captain that did bring me first on shore
Hath my maid's garments. He upon some action
Is now in durance, at Malvolio's suit,
A gentleman, and follower of my lady's.
OLIVIA: He shall enlarge him. Fetch Malvolio hither;

272 *a . . . extracting frenzy,* a passion that drew me from myself.

275 *Belzebub,* Satan.

278–9 *epistles . . . delivered.* An elaborate set of quibbles on 'epistles', 'gospels', 'delivered'.

Madmen's letters are not works of truth (just as everybody knows that New Testament Epistles are not Gospels), and therefore the time of delivering them is unimportant. On the other hand it is important that the Epistle or Gospel 'appointed for the day' should be delivered (i.e. read) at the proper day and time in the Communion Service.

282 *By the Lord, madam.* Feste imitates a madman. How?

285 *allow Vox,* allow the appropriate pitch and volume in my voice.

288 *perpend, . . . ear.* Perhaps a hint of Sir Topas in his voice and a recollection of Psalm 45, 'Hearken, O daughter, and consider and incline thine ear'.

Feste has no intention of reading sensibly. How does Fabian get hold of the letter?

What qualities belong to the writer of the letter: sincerity, scorn, loyalty, sense of duty, clear mind, outraged dignity, pomposity, contempt, madness, injured innocence?

And yet, alas, now I remember me,
They say, poor gentleman, he's much distract.

*Enter* FESTE *with a letter, and* FABIAN

A most extracting frenzy of mine own
From my remembrance clearly banished his.
How does he, sirrah?

FESTE: Truly, madam, he holds Belzebub at the stave's end as well as a man in his case may do. Has here writ a letter to you. I should have given't you today morning, but as a madman's epistles are no gospels, so it skills not much when they are delivered.

OLIVIA: Open 't, and read it.

FESTE: Look then to be well edified when the fool delivers the madman. [*Reads*] 'By the Lord, madam'—

OLIVIA: How now! Art thou mad?

FESTE: No, madam, I do but read madness. An your ladyship will have it as it ought to be, you must allow Vox.

OLIVIA: Prithee read i' thy right wits.

FESTE: So I do, madonna; but to read his right wits is to read thus. Therefore perpend, my princess, and give ear.

OLIVIA: [*To Fabian*] Read it you, sirrah.

FABIAN: [*Reads*] 'By the Lord, madam, you wrong me, and the world shall know it. Though you have put me into darkness and given your drunken cousin rule over me, yet have I the benefit of my senses as well as your ladyship. I have your own letter that induced me to the semblance I put on, with the which I doubt not but to do myself much right or you much shame. Think of me as you please. I leave my duty a little unthought of, and speak out of my injury.

THE MADLY-USED MALVOLIO.'

OLIVIA: Did he write this?

FESTE: Ay, madam.

DUKE: This savours not much of distraction.

303 This is a continuation of the conversation before the references to Malvolio.

306 *proper cost*, own expense.

308 *quits*, frees.

319 *from it*, differently.

320 *invention*, style of phrasing.

OLIVIA: See him delivered, Fabian; bring him hither.
[*Exit Fabian*
My lord, so please you, these things further thought on,
To think me as well a sister as a wife,
One day shall crown th' alliance on't, so please you,
Here at my house and at my proper cost.
DUKE: Madam, I am most apt t' embrace your offer.
[*To Viola*] Your master quits you; and for your service done him,
So much against the mettle of your sex,
So far beneath your soft and tender breeding,
And since you called me master for so long,
Here is my hand: you shall from this time be
Your master's mistress.
OLIVIA: A sister, you are she.
*Enter* FABIAN *with* MALVOLIO
DUKE: Is this the madman?
OLIVIA: Ay, my lord, this same.
How now, Malvolio?
MALVOLIO: Madam, you have done me wrong,
Notorious wrong.
OLIVIA: Have I, Malvolio? No.
MALVOLIO: Lady, you have. Pray you peruse that letter.
You must not now deny it is your hand;
Write from it if you can, in hand or phrase;
Or say 'tis not your seal, not your invention;
You can say none of this. Well, grant it then,
And tell me, in the modesty of honour,
Why you have given me such clear lights of favour,
Bade me come smiling and cross-gartered to you,
To put on yellow stockings and to frown
Upon Sir Toby and the lighter people;
And, acting this in an obedient hope,
Why have you suffered me to be imprisoned,

330 *geck,* fool.

333 *character,* handwriting.

337–8 *presupposed Upon thee,* suggested to you beforehand.

339 *practice,* trick.
*shrewdly passed upon,* cunningly made a fool of.

340–2 A generous offer to put right Malvolio's wrongs.

345 *which . . . at,* which I see with surprise and admiration.

349 *conceived . . . him,* perceived in him.

350 *importance,* importunity, urging.

352 *sportful malice.* Do you agree?

353 *pluck,* bring.

356 *poor fool.* An expression of pity. *baffled,* humiliated. An ironic echo. (See II. v, 143-4.)

359 *interlude,* play.

Kept in a dark house, visited by the priest,
And made the most notorious geck and gull
That e'er invention played on? Tell me why.

OLIVIA: Alas, Malvolio, this is not my writing,
Though, I confess, much like the character;
But out of question 'tis Maria's hand.
And now I do bethink me, it was she
First told me thou wast mad; thou camest in smiling,
And in such forms which here were presupposed
Upon thee in the letter. Prithee be content,
This practice hath most shrewdly passed upon thee.
But when we know the grounds and authors of it,
Thou shalt be both the plaintiff and the judge
Of thine own cause.

FABIAN: Good madam, hear me speak,
And let no quarrel nor no brawl to come
Taint the condition of this present hour,
Which I have wondered at. In hope it shall not,
Most freely I confess myself and Toby
Set this device against Malvolio here,
Upon some stubborn and uncourteous parts
We had conceived against him. Maria writ
The letter at Sir Toby's great importance,
In recompense whereof he hath married her.
How with a sportful malice it was followed,
May rather pluck on laughter than revenge,
If that the injuries be justly weighed
That have on both sides passed.

OLIVIA: Alas, poor fool, how have they baffled thee!

FESTE: Why, 'Some are born great, some achieve greatness, and some have greatness thrown upon them.' I was one, sir in this interlude, one Sir Topas, sir; but that's all one. 'By the Lord, fool, I am not mad.' But do you remember?—'Madam why laugh you at such a barren rascal? An you smile not

362 *whirligig of time.* Time brings about changes in fortune. The turning of Fortune's Wheel was thought to account for the sudden changes from prosperity to wretchedness or vice versa. The belief underlies this phrase of Feste.

Which of these epithets suit Feste: malicious, justified, callous, jealous, unkind, moralizing, unpleasant, light-hearted?

364 *I'll . . . you.* Has Malvolio's punishment been too great?

365 *notoriously abused.* Olivia quotes Malvolio. Is she laughing?

368 *convents,* brings us together.

377 *A foolish . . . toy,* my follies were mere child's play.

389 *toss-pots,* drunkards.

Is this a pathetic song or are the verses interludes in a jig? (See Appendix III.)

he's gagged'. And thus the whirligig of time brings in his revenges.

MALVOLIO: I'll be revenged on the whole pack of you. [*Exit*

OLIVIA: He hath been most notoriously abused.

DUKE: Pursue him, and entreat him to a peace;
He hath not told us of the captain yet.
When that is known and golden time convents,
A solemn combination shall be made
Of our dear souls. Meantime, sweet sister,
We will not part from hence. Cesario, come—
For so you shall be, while you are a man—
But when in other habits you are seen,
Orsino's mistress and his fancy's queen.

[*Exeunt all, except Feste*

FESTE: [*Sings*]

When that I was and a little tiny boy
  With hey, ho, the wind and the rain,
A foolish thing was but a toy,
  For the rain it raineth every day.

But when I came to man's estate,
  With hey, ho, &c.
'Gainst knaves and thieves men shut their gate,
  For the rain, &c.

But when I came, alas, to wive,
  With hey, ho, &c.
By swaggering could I never thrive,
  For the rain, &c.

But when I came unto my beds,
  With hey, ho, &c.
With toss-pots still had drunken heads,
  For the rain, &c.

A great while ago the world begun,
  With hey, ho, &c.
But that's all one, our play is done,
  And we'll strive to please you every day. [*Exit*

# APPENDICES

## I

## THE DATE OF TWELFTH NIGHT

FROM evidence not connected with the royal occasion of 1601 we know that *Twelfth Night* was written between 1598, or perhaps 1600, and 2 February, 1602, dates that are quite consistent with a performance in 1601. The evidence, however, that links the play to the Twelfth Night celebrations at Court is impressive and convincing.

Shakespeare does not name any of his other plays after a festival, and his plays do not usually have an alternative title, certainly not his other comedies. In the absence of any direct reference to Twelfth Night in the play, and at a time when the feast was marked with such traditional revelry, it is inconceivable that it should be so named unless its first performance took place on that feast day. At a guess it may have been presented first as *What You Will,* a title in keeping with *Much Ado About Nothing, All's Well That Ends Well,* and *As You Like It* and then as the Twelfth Night play its outstanding success may have inspired the additional title, *Twelfth Night,* as a memorable honour and a profitable advertisement.

The use of Orsino as the name of an important character in the play seems clearly intended as a compliment to the Queen's guest; such a compliment would have point only if Orsino were at the performance to receive it.

Again, a number of phrases and obscure allusions in the text take on an intelligibility and vivid life if interpreted in the light of a Court performance in the Great Hall.

Finally, the Lord Chamberlain, Lord Hunsdon, the patron of Shakespeare's company, was himself charged with requisitioning a play for that evening. He would certainly have invited his own players to present a play, which, as he anxiously noted, 'shalbe best furnished with rich apparell. have greate variety and change of Musicke and daunces, and of a subject that may be most pleasing to her Maiestie'. The company did in fact act at Court on that date since a payment was made to them for so doing.

He was further required to 'appoint Musicke severally for the Queene, and some for the play in the Hall. And Hales to have one place expressly to shewe his owne voyce'. The lutanist, Hales, was the finest singer of his day. Now in Act II Scene 4 Orsino asks Viola for the 'song . . . we heard last night', and he is told that Feste, who sang it, is not there, and Curio is sent to find him. This may well be the place in which Hales, not on the acting floor, was courteously led forward by Curio to 'shewe his owne voyce' in 'Come away death'. For public performance Feste sang the song, but the method of introducing Hales was retained.

Dr. Hotson believes that the play was written, rehearsed and presented within a fortnight, a feat reported of at least three other plays of the period. On the other hand to perform at Court was the ambition of all the companies, and as Twelfth Night was the most important occasion in the year for the production of plays at Court, it is most unlikely that Shakespeare's company, aware that other companies were rehearsing plays avowedly for this festival, would have no play in preparation. In any case *Twelfth Night* shows no signs of hasty composition, though it does show signs of revision. It may, therefore, have been written well beforehand with Court performance on Twelfth Night in mind. Only minor modifications would then be necessary to fit it for the special circumstances at Court in 1601.

## II

## SHAKESPEARE'S THEATRE

THE first public theatres in London were built during Shakespeare's lifetime, but they embodied in their design and construction the experience and practice of the medieval and Tudor play productions in inn yards and elsewhere.

From square, circular or hexagonal theatre walls tiered with galleries for spectators the Elizabethan stage jutted out over six feet above ground level and occupied about half the floor space where the spectators could stand on three sides of it. The stage of the Fortune theatre was 43 feet × 27 feet and the floor area in which it stood was 55 feet × 55 feet. At the back of the stage the lowest tier of spectators' galleries gave place to a curtained recess or inner stage used for interior scenes. On either side were dressing rooms from which entrance doors opened on to the stage. The first floor gallery behind the stage was used as a balcony for musicians or for scenes in the play; if it was not required for these purposes, spectators used it. Above the balcony and covering the rear portion of the stage was a canopy or roof painted blue and adorned with stars supported by pillars from the stage. There were trap doors in the stage and frequently a low rail around it.

The pillars, canopy, railings and back stage were painted and adorned. If a tragedy was to be performed, the stage was hung with black, but there was no set staging in the modern fashion.

There were stage properties usually of the kind that could be easily pushed on and off the stage. Records of the time mention a mossy bank, a wall, a bed, trees, arbours, thrones, tents, rock, tomb, hell-mouth, a cauldron; on the other hand pavilions and mansions may have been permanent 'sets' in some historical plays. On the whole properties were limited to essentials although the popularity of the private masques with their painted canvas sets encouraged increasing elaboration of scenery and spectacle during the reign of James I.

There was no limitation to the display of rich and gorgeous costumes in the current fashion of the day. The more magnificent and splendid the better; indeed the costumes must have been the most expensive item in the requirements of the company. An occasional attempt was made at period costume, but normally plays were produced in Elizabethan garments without any suspicion of the oddness that strikes us when we read of Caesar entering 'in his nightshirt' or Cleopatra calling on Charmian to cut the lace of what we may call her corsets. High rank was marked by magnificence of dress, a trade or calling by functional clothes. Feste, the clown, would wear the traditional fool's coat or petticoat of motley, a coarse cloth of mixed yellow and green. The coat was buttoned from the neck to the girdle from which hung a wooden dagger, its skirts voluminous with capacious pockets in which Feste might 'impetticoat' any 'gratillity'. Ghosts, who appear in a number of plays, wore a kind of leathern smock. Oberon and magicians

The Globe Theatre
A reconstruction by Dr J. C. Adams and Irwin Smith

such as Prospero wore, in the delightful phrase and spelling of the records, 'a robe for to goo invisibell'.

The actors formed companies under the patronage of noblemen for protection against a civic law condemning them as 'rogues, vagabonds and sturdy beggars' to severe punishment. They were the servants of their patron, and wore his livery. The company was a co-operative society, its members jointly owned the property and shared the profits; thus Shakespeare's plays were not his to use as he liked, they belonged to his company, the Lord Chamberlain's Men. This company, honoured by James I when it became the King's Men, was the most successful company of the period. It had a number of distinguished actors, it achieved more Court performances than any other company, and it performed in the best London theatre, the Globe, until it was burnt down during a performance of *Henry VIII* in 1613. Women were not allowed on the public stage, although they performed in masques and theatricals in private houses. Boys, therefore, were apprenticed to the leading actors and took the female parts.

The audience in the public theatres was drawn from all classes. There were courtiers and inns of court men who appreciated intricate word play, mythological allusions and the technique of sword play; there were the 'groundlings' who liked jigs, horse-play and flamboyance of speech and spectacle; and there were the citizens who appreciated the romantic stories, the high eloquence of patriotic plays and moral sentiments. A successful play would have something for all. Sometimes gallants would sit on a stool on the stage and behave rather like the courtiers in *A Midsummer Night's Dream,* V. i, or *Love's Labour's Lost,* V. ii. The 'groundlings' too were likely to be troublesome and noisy. They could buy bottled-beer, oranges and nuts for their comfort; but it is noted to their credit that when Falstaff appeared on the stage, so popular was he that they stopped cracking nuts! They applauded a well-delivered speech; they hissed a boring play; they even rioted and severely damaged one theatre. Shakespeare's plays however were popular among all classes: at Court they

did so take Eliza and our James,

and elsewhere in the public theatre they outshone the plays of other dramatists. Any play of his was assured of a 'full house'. As for *Twelfth*

*Night*, particularly the gulling of Malvolio, it appealed to them all high and low and Charles I was so far impressed as to write 'Malvolio' beside the play in his copy of Shakespeare now at Windsor Castle and an ardent theatre-goer of the day wrote

lo in a trice
The cockpit, galleries, boxes, all are full
To hear Malvolio, that cross-garter'd gull.

## III

## MUSIC IN TWELFTH NIGHT

TWELFTH NIGHT begins in music, it ends in song, and throughout song and music break in with charming freshness and spontaneity. Its prelude of instrumental music was played originally perhaps by a small orchestra of about six players in a combination of recorders, viols or lutes, what the Elizabethans called a 'broken consort'. Such an arrangement of instruments would have produced the soft, sweet music appropriate to Orsino's mood. The music they played, however, is not known. Orsino's love-languishing mood continues during his next appearance (II. iv) and again his household musicians underline it by the softly played tune to 'Come away, come away, death'. On his third appearance in the last scene there is no soft music; he has at last been roused to action.

It is Feste's group of songs, leaving out the ballad 'Hey, Robin', that have set their seal on the play. Their variety, their apt relation to the situation or to the moods of those to whom Feste sings give them a subtle choric quality. The tender simplicity of 'O mistress mine' with its sentimental appeal to the two tipsy knights inspires them in good fellowship, in the warmth of their wine-glad hearts, to rouse the night owl—and the household.

'Come away, come away, death' exquisitely matches Orsino's melancholy. It is the perennial lament of the unrequited lover in folk song and ballad arranged here in a more elaborate verse form. Unfortunately its tune that gave 'a very echo to the seat where love is throned' has been lost.

At the end of IV. ii, with his jingling song, 'I am gone, sir' Feste recalls the character of the Vice in the morality plays who with clowning and horse-play beat and drove the devil into hell. Feste, agreeing to help Malvolio, perhaps burlesqued the actions of the Vice as he sang, and pretended to belabour and drive away the devil by whom Malvolio was supposed to be possessed.

His epilogue, 'When that I was' has a sentimental fascination for modern audiences who read into it the pathos of the Clown who loved his lady in vain. Alternatively it can be taken as a vagabond song with a hint of roguery and knavery. The pupil may choose whether he takes it as a pathetic little ditty near to tears for the sadness of things, or whether he takes it, accompanied by a jig, as Feste's final, impudent chuckle over his own naughtiness.

There is little to say about the catches and songs sung by the revellers in II. iii, they are the popular songs of the day. Hotson, however, sees in 'There dwelt a man in Babylon' and the reference to Peg-a-Ramsey allusions to Sir William Knollys.

Here are some notes on the words and music of the songs in the order of their occurrence.

II. iii, 36 *O mistress mine*

The words may be Shakespeare's re-writing of a popular song to be sung to the original tune. The original tune, now lost, may have been the basis of a tune named 'O mistress mine' by Thomas Morley. As it stands Morley's tune does not quite fit the words, but it has been suitably arranged by modern composers.

II. iii, 60 *Hold thy peace, thou knave*
*And I prithee hold thy peace*

The tune is printed in Long's *Shakespeare's Use of Music*, p. 173.

II. iii, 70 *Three merry men, and three merry men,*
*And three merry men be we:*
*I in the wood and thou on the ground,*
*And Jack sleeps in the tree.*

Words from Peel's *Old Wives' Tale*, 1595; tune from Playford's *Dancing Master*, 1650.

II. iii, 72 *There dwelt a man in Babylon*
*Of reputation great by fame;*
*He took to wife a fair woman,*
*Susanna she was called by name.*
*A woman fair and virtuous:*
*Lady, lady!*
*Why should we not of her learn thus*
*To live godly?*

*The Ballad of Constant Susanna* quoted from Percy's *Reliques*. The story is the well-known one of Susanna and the Elders from the *Apocrypha*. The tune is a variant form of 'Greensleeves'.

II. iii, 93 *Farewell dear heart*

Sir Toby and Feste adapt this song very neatly to discomfort Malvolio. The original words relevant to the scene are:

*Farewell dear love, since thou wilt needs be gone,*
*Mine eyes do show my life is almost done.*
*Nay, I will never die*
*So long as I can spy*
. . . . . .
*Shall I bid her go?*
*What and if I do?*
*Shall I bid her go and spare not?*
*O no, no, no, no, no, I dare not.*

The rejected lover consoles himself with the thought that there are other ladies; but in the last line his resolution fails him, and he dare not let his lady go.

Words and tune are from Robert Jones' *First Book of Songs and Airs*, 1600.

II. iv, 51 *Come away, come away, death*

Nothing more is known of this song.

IV. ii, 69 *A Robin, gentle Robin,*
*Tell me how thy leman doth,*
*And thou shalt know of mine.*
*My lady is unkind, I wis*
*Alack, why is she so?*

*She loveth another better than me*
*And yet she will say no.*

From a manuscript, Additional 31922 f 54, in the British Museum.

IV. ii, 113 *I am gone, sir*

This may be intended as a piece of extempore singing by Feste.

V. i, 375 *When that I was*

It is thought that the comedian and ballad-maker Robert Armin who took Feste's part composed these verses. The origin of the traditional tune is not known.

ROBERT ARMIN
Shakespeare's Feste

# IV

## MALVOLIO AND MARIA

The steward was the most important official in the Elizabethan aristocratic household. He was himself a gentleman by birth, often a knight, and under his direction were a number of gentlemen servants and gentlewomen-in-waiting together with a larger number of yeomen-servants, maids, laundresses, grooms, porters, boys and casual workers. He was responsible to his lord or lady for the organization and running of the household. He appointed and dismissed servants, he arranged for the supply of provisions, the issue of liveries and payment of wages, the checking of accounts and stores, and he received the guests. To assist him in the various sections of the household were the Controller, the Gentleman of the Horse, the Gentleman Usher, the Clerk of the Kitchen. All the orders and statutes set down by his lord he read openly to the servants once a quarter to see that they were known.

He was responsible for discipline, and in some households he consulted with the Gentleman Usher, the Chaplain, the Gentleman of the Horse, and the Clerk of the Kitchen every Friday evening on the maintenance of good conduct among the servants. In Viscount Montague's *Book of Orders,* quoted by Miss St. Clare Byrne, the Steward was instructed to 'reprehend and correct the negligent and disordered persons and reform them by his grave admonitions and vigilant eye over them, the riotous, the contentious, and the quarrelous persons of any degree . . . the frequenters of tabling, carding, and dicing in corners and at untimely hours and seasons'.

He dressed in a dignified manner befitting one who carried so much responsibility. He wore a rich robe often trimmed with fur, a gold-plated chain often with a jewel attached hung round his neck and carried a silver-headed staff of office.

Malvolio's ambition to marry Olivia was not therefore in itself such an impossibility. Indeed Miss St. Clare Byrne draws attention to this point:

'The fantastic fun that as a rule we extract from the gulling of Malvolio gets an abrupt shock at his final exit. There is sharper comedy, more in keeping with that troublesome exit, if we realise that, in Elizabethan fact, the gulling of Malvolio hovers perpetually on the brink of reason, the verge of reality. Katharine Willoughby, Dowager Duchess of Suffolk, married as her second husband Richard Bertie, her Gentleman-Usher! She was one of the romantic figures of the age, and the story of her life was as widely known as Foxe's *Book of Martyrs*—second only to the Bible in its popularity—could make it. Her step-daughter, Frances Duchess of Suffolk, married her Groom of the Chamber, Adrian Stokes; and Lady Mary Grey—daughter of Frances, and step-granddaughter of Katharine—who stood in the direct succession to the throne, actually married the Queen's Sergeant-Porter. "There is example for it: the lady of the Strachy married the yeoman of the wardrobe." '

Malvolio's puritanism mentioned by Maria and then reduced to time-pleaser, affectioned ass is lightly sketched. He disapproves of cakes and ale and of the licensed fool, he is self-righteous and devoid of a sense of proportion. Perhaps the edge of the jest to an Elizabethan audience is that one so righteous and so sure that he is divinely and astrologically favoured should be thought to be possessed of a devil!

Malvolio may have been drawn from life, and William Farington, Lord Derby's steward, has been suggested as a model. However, it is only if the portrait is a caricature recognized by the audience that it becomes dramatically significant. Two candidates for this honour have been put forward, Sir Ambrose Willoughby, Chief Server to the Queen, and Sir William Knollys. Sir Edward Chambers identified Malvolio with Knollys, and Hotson amplified the suggestion into a full satirical portrait.

Sir William Knollys, a member of a puritan family from Banbury, represented that town in Parliament. He became infatuated with Mary (Mall) Fitton, one of Queen Elizabeth's maids of honour, and this brought ridicule upon him. The name 'Malvolio' may be a quibble, 'ill-will' or 'I want Mall'. Hotson finds a number of possible allusions to Knollys: puritanism, cakes and ale (famous in Banbury), the aptness to Knollys of the Peg-a-Ramsey ballad refrain, the 'colour of his beard' (Knollys attempted to dye his) and others less convincing.

Maria, too, should be regarded as a gentlewoman and not as a kind of barmaid. She is a gentlewoman-in-waiting, a person of gentle birth and upbringing. The trio Maria, Sir Toby and Sir Andrew occupy a somewhat higher ranking in Elizabethan estimation than we are inclined to allow them.

J. Nichols, *History and Antiquities of Leicestershire*, 1804. Vol. III, p. 594. Gladys S. Thomson, *Life in a Noble Household*, 1641-1700, 1950. Muriel St. Clare Byrne, 'The Social Background' (*Companion to Shakespeare Studies*, 1934).

## *Shakespeare's Works*

The year of composition of only a few of Shakespeare's plays can be determined with certainty. The following list is based on current scholarly opinion.

The plays marked with an asterisk were not included in the First Folio edition of Shakespeare's plays (1623) which was prepared by Heminge and Condell, Shakespeare's fellow actors. Shakespeare's part in them has been much debated.

| | |
|---|---|
| 1590–1 | 2 Henry VI, 3 Henry VI. |
| 1591–2 | 1 Henry VI. |
| 1592–3 | Richard III, Comedy of Errors. |
| 1593–4 | Titus Andronicus, Taming of the Shrew, Sir Thomas More* (Part authorship. Four manuscript pages presumed to be in Shakespeare's hand). |
| 1594–5 | Two Gentlemen of Verona, Love's Labour's Lost, Romeo and Juliet, Edward III* (Part authorship). |
| 1595–6 | Richard II, A Midsummer Night's Dream. |
| 1596–7 | King John, Merchant of Venice, Love's Labour Won (Not extant. Before 1598). |
| 1597–8 | 1 Henry IV, 2 Henry IV, The Merry Wives of Windsor. |
| 1598–9 | Much Ado About Nothing, Henry V. |
| 1599–1600 | Julius Caesar, As You Like It. |
| 1600–1 | Hamlet, Twelfth Night. |
| 1601–2 | Troilus and Cressida. |
| 1602–3 | All's Well that Ends Well. |